TRAIL

OF

TERROR

About the Author

Richard Estep (Boulder, CO) first got involved with paranormal research in 1995 in the UK after attending an overnight investigation at the infamous St. Botolph's ("Skidbrooke") church. He spent the next five years investigating the haunted hamlets of Great Britain as a member of Andrew Wright's Leicester-based team. Richard cofounded Boulder County Paranormal Research Society (BCPRS) with his wife, Laura, after relocating to the United States in 1999. Richard's work has been featured on the TV shows *Haunted Case Files* and *Haunted Hospitals*. Visit him online at http://www.richardestep.net/.

RICHARD ESTEP

TRAIL

OF

TERROR

**THE BLACK MONK OF PONTEFRACT,
CRIPPLE CREEK JAIL,
FIREHOUSE PHANTOM,
AND OTHER TRUE HAUNTINGS**

Llewellyn Publications
Woodbury, Minnesota

FIRST EDITION
First Printing, 2018

Cover design by Kevin R. Brown
Interior photos provided by the author

Llewellyn Publications is a registered trademark of Llewellyn Worldwide Ltd.

Library of Congress Cataloging-in-Publication Data

Names: Estep, Richard, author.

Title: Trail of terror : the Black Monk of Pontefract, Cripple Creek Jail, firehouse phantom, and other true hauntings / Richard Estep.

Description: First edition. | Woodbury, MN : Llewellyn Publications, [2018].

Identifiers: LCCN 2018024773 (print) | LCCN 2018037136 (ebook) | ISBN

9780738756134 (ebook) | ISBN 9780738756066 | ISBN 9780738756066(alk. paper)

Subjects: LCSH: Ghosts. | Haunted places.

Classification: LCC BF1461 (ebook) | LCC BF1461 .E88 2018 (print) | DDC

133.1—dc23

LC record available at https://lccn.loc.gov/2018024773

Llewellyn Worldwide Ltd. does not participate in, endorse, or have any authority or responsibility concerning private business transactions between our authors and the public.

All mail addressed to the author is forwarded, but the publisher cannot, unless specifically instructed by the author, give out an address or phone number.

Any internet references contained in this work are current at publication time, but the publisher cannot guarantee that a specific location will continue to be maintained. Please refer to the publisher's website for links to authors' websites and other sources.

Llewellyn Publications
A Division of Llewellyn Worldwide Ltd.
2143 Wooddale Drive
Woodbury, MN 55125-2989
www.llewellyn.com

Printed in the United States of America

Other Books by Richard Estep

Dedicated to Jack Stackpool for his love and support.
'Tis himself, he is. Much love, Mike Stackpool.

Contents

FOREWORD

There are strange things in this world. Impossible things. Things we see just out of the corner of our eye. Things that go bump in the night. Things we are told as children that we should not believe in.

As human beings, we have evolved to fear such things. To be wary of the dark places and the shadows. To stay upon the lighted paths and stray not into those places that the strange things might call home. For we find safety and peace in the light, and we find comfort in telling ourselves that the strange things are not real. That there is nothing in that darkness to fear.

There are some humans who ignore this evolutionary advice, though. Where others see darkness and fear, they see the mystery of the strange things and seek to know what truly lingers in the shadows. They seek out the darkness and the things that reside within it. Some would call such people fools or weirdos, but the people who find this calling prefer to be known as investigators.

For that is what they truly are. These souls seek not the thrill of the darkness and the fear it may contain, but they seek to know what truly resides there.

These people leave the places of light and comfort to wander the cold and dark places of the world in search of answers. They seek the truth to the old legends and tales of hauntings and strangeness. Perhaps by doing so they bring a light of their own into that darkness.

Sometimes that light shines back out into the world of the normal, for in visiting that dark place, they find some reasonable explanation for the strangeness and give us all the comfort of knowing that the moaning that once came from an old house was nothing more than a door creaking on ancient hinges when the wind blew. Sometimes they find that the place they dared enter had no activity at all. That whatever strangeness was said to be had long since ended.

There are times, however, when these investigators find the strange thing they are seeking, and they witness things that the normal will refuse to believe. They hold conversations with the darkness and they receive answers. They confront the strangeness, and they return again and again to seek a glimpse of a world that for most is ever unseen.

You are about to walk the trail of terror.

You are about to follow the investigations of a man who has peered into more dark places than most and sought the answers to those questions we mostly fear to ask.

What lies in the shadows? What really does go bump in the night?

I have known this man for some time and invite you to sit back and let him take you on this journey to explore the unknown. Walk those halls with him from the comfort of wherever you now are, and he will take you safely into the shadows and deliver you safely back to the light. Be not afraid, but may you wander and wonder with my dear friend Richard Estep.

—Aiden Sinclair, Illusionist

INTRODUCTION

When I first began to investigate claims of ghostly encounters and haunted houses during the midnineties, the field of paranormal investigation looked significantly different from how it looks today. For starters, we lacked the plethora of television shows covering the subject that are now so popular.

I drifted into paranormal field research after a lifelong interest in all things of that nature, learning investigative techniques from other enthusiastic amateurs as we went along. Our tool kit was very basic and easily affordable. A notebook and pen, a flashlight, a tape recorder with spare cassettes, and a plentiful supply of caffeinated beverages were pretty much all it took to get out there and start looking for answers. We really felt that we had "arrived" when we were finally able to afford a VHS camcorder and a tripod to mount it on.

Contrast that with the dizzying array of equipment available to the paranormal enthusiast today. I have friends who have spent the better part of a year's salary on their inventory, stocking up on banks of remote cameras, forward-looking infrared (FLIR) imagers, and a host of technological wizardry the likes of which would turn a CIA agent green with envy. (Yes, I exaggerate—but only a little.)

What has most decidedly not changed in the years since then—indeed, since the inception of paranormal research during the nineteenth century—is the single most important tool of all: a critical mind. When the Society for Psychical Research (SPR) first began to systematically study accounts of apparitions, visions, psychic mediumship, poltergeist activity, and other similarly fascinating claims, they lacked any semblance of the sophisticated technology available to today's field researcher. What they substituted instead was a thorough understanding of the scientific method, the ingrained ability to set a high standard for what constituted evidence and to test its validity using all ingenious means at their disposal.

The willingness to discard potential evidence based upon its flimsy nature does not come easily to most of us. It is only natural for the enthusiastic ghost hunter to want those creaking floorboards to be caused by the tread of some phantom, after all. We spend hours, sometimes days, in semidarkness of a property, seeking to capture elusive evidence of paranormal activity taking place. Packing up one's equipment and leaving empty-handed when the sun comes up the next morning tends to feel like failure, as though our precious time has been squandered. Far easier and more comforting to fall into the comfortable trap of assuming that the garbled static captured by the digital voice recorder is in fact an intelligible electronic voice phenomenon (EVP) placed there by a discarnate entity who wishes to communicate with us.

As you read the stories in this book, accompanying my team and me on investigations of some of the most fascinating locations on either side of the Atlantic, please bear one thing in mind: there is no commonly accepted standard for what constitutes evidence of the paranormal. What one person may believe is absolutely proof of the existence of ghosts, spirits, or other discarnate entities will easily be written off by another as nothing more than an overly credulous imagination.

The purpose of this book is not to try and change or challenge your belief system. We live in a huge and mysterious universe, with plenty of room for all manner of perspectives. Just like you, I have my own beliefs and biases, which I freely admit lean very much in favor of the reality of paranormal phenomena. I ask only that you read with an open mind.

One of the best-kept open secrets of our field is this: ghost hunting is usually pretty boring. At least 90 percent of the time is spent setting up equipment, monitoring that equipment while waiting for something to happen, breaking down and repacking that equipment, and finally reviewing the hours and hours of data that the equipment recorded in the form of video camera footage, still photo images, and audio recordings.

It is a strange and fascinating time to be involved in the field of paranormal investigation, and after looking back on the cases I have documented in this book, I can't help but wonder what the next twenty years will bring. Hopefully they will be every bit as exciting as the last two decades have been!

CHAPTER 1

JAILHOUSE ROCK

Over the years, I've found that one of the weirder perks of being a paranormal investigator seems to be that you get to spend more than your fair share of nights locked up in prisons and jails of various descriptions—albeit with the added bonus that they usually let you out the next day! I once spent five days living in an ancient prison for those accused of witchcraft whose original structure dates back to the English witch trials of the 1500s.

There is something deeply fascinating about walking the hallways and being locked inside the cells of such places of incarceration. Even so many years after they were abandoned, their final prisoners having been discharged or moved on to other facilities, a sense of despair and tragic isolation hangs over such places; it is often so strong as to be almost palpable, which should come as no surprise when one considers the amount of sheer misery (often coupled with acts of unspeakably brutal violence) that those walls have seen over the years.

So what could possibly be better than spending the night inside a mountain town's old jail, one that dates back to the era of the gold rush? Why, doing it to help out a good cause, of course. When my friend Colton Tapia of the Eastern Colorado Shadow Trackers contacted me and offered me the opportunity to be part of an overnight investigation in a mining town named Cripple Creek, whose primary source of revenue was now its tourism, casinos, and hotels, I immediately jumped at the chance.

Colton's plans were both ambitious and laudable. Far too often the paranormal research community is rife with political infighting and backbiting, with some groups being extremely territorial about what they perceive to be "their" locations. To his great credit, Colton's approach was the very opposite: he intended to bring together several different teams, each with their own unique approaches to investigating, their own blends of equipment and personnel. Everybody would get a piece of the pie, having the opportunity to move throughout the old jail throughout the course of the evening, working with one another in order to achieve a greater goal.

The jail (now the Outlaw and Lawmen Museum) was to be wired up with multiple cameras, each of which fed sound and images back toward a command center that Colton had set up in the gift shop. Banks of monitors displayed the camera output, which he was also streaming out live across the internet. His idea was that armchair paranormal enthusiasts would be able to tune in, watch the investigation as it happened in real time, and hopefully donate to one of the several charities that the event was intended to support.

It was a brilliant idea, and one that both I and my colleague Dr. Catlyn Keenan were only too happy to be a part of. Catlyn spends the working week immersed in the world of academia, teaching a wide variety of courses at a community college. Her almost encyclopedic knowledge of the world's many religions and faiths had proved to be a valuable asset to the team on more than one occasion, and I was delighted to have her along with me as a fellow representative of the Boulder County Paranormal Research Society (BCPRS).

After a long drive along winding mountainous roads, some of which had treacherous hairpin bends and drop-offs so steep that they were almost vertical, we finally hit Cripple Creek and made our way directly to the old jail. Two stories tall and constructed of red brick that looks a lot newer than its actual age of 110 years, the jail is shaped like the letter T. Stout metal bars cover all the windows, which went some way toward explaining why the jail had such a reputation of security. Very few prisoners were ever able to bust their way out successfully.

The parking lot was full of people when we arrived, either unloading cases of equipment or talking animatedly with one another in small clusters. I was pleased to see a number of old friends, and before the night was over, I would be fortunate enough to have made one or two new ones.

I spent some time catching up with those people I knew and making the acquaintance of those I didn't. We took a walk-through of the property, which had appeared deceptively small from the outside. Once through the gift shop and into the jail proper, we found the multistory cellblock, encased within the main structure of the building. There was also the opportunity to learn a little about the town's history and the jail's place within it.

Blood and Gold

The gold rush struck Colorado on more than one occasion, and mining towns such as Cripple Creek sprang up all across the state, wherever there was even a hint of gold fever. Most began as little more than small encampments, and some never outgrew that label; yet others managed to become townships in their own right, duly attracting the multitude of support services that were necessary to keep the hardworking gold miners happy—which basically meant liquor, gambling, and prostitutes.

The jail had once served all of Teller County, not just the township of Cripple Creek itself, which made for a steady flow of inmates passing through its cells. If the ghost stories were true, some of them may never have left when the jail closed its doors officially for the last time in 1991.

Coming from relatively humble origins, Cripple Creek's population suddenly exploded when the mines became a success, going from double digits to more than fifty thousand at the dawn of the twentieth century. Although fairly calm during the day when most of the menfolk were away working in the mines, the town became something entirely different when the sun went down. Mining is a hard and dangerous business, and most miners were hard-drinking, hard-fighting men. They descended on the saloons and brothels en masse every night, usually with a fistful of dollars burning a hole in their pocket and a great deal of frustration to be worked off.

By 1901 the town had grown large enough to require the services of a courthouse and a jail with which to keep it fed with a steady supply of miscreants. Unlike some of the bigger cities, life in and around the mining towns could be harsh, brutal... and short. It wasn't uncommon for disputes to be settled with fists, feet, blades, and even guns in some cases.

The old Cripple Creek jail, which is now a museum.

As I was walking around the old jail, I stopped at regular intervals to read the many signs that had been posted by the museum staff. They detailed the history of Cripple Creek and its surroundings, including some of the more brutal crimes which had taken place. One particularly fascinating case was the 1901 murder of a fellow named Sam Strong who made a small fortune in the local mining industry. Overly fond of booze, gambling, and ladies of negotiable affection, Strong had racked up a huge debt at the Newport Saloon. When its owner, one Grant Crumley, had insisted on repayment, Strong had responded by writing him a check ... on which he promptly stopped payment.

Enraged, the saloon owner was all ready to go looking for payback when his debtor obligingly walked through the doors of the Newport and staggered up to face him. Strong was as drunk as a lord, which wouldn't have helped his aim when he whipped out a pistol and stuck it in the astonished Crumley's face. Crumley was quick enough to take cover behind the bar, and when he emerged, it was Strong's turn to be surprised: the enraged saloon owner was wielding a shotgun, which he promptly aimed in the direction of Strong's head and pulled the trigger.

In the long run, few truly dangerous prisoners were kept in the Cripple Creek jail for any great length of time: being a jail rather than a prison, it wasn't really equipped to handle them for very long. Those who were considered to be a true threat ended up serving their time in the Colorado Territorial Prison at Canon City, which was much better prepared to deal with the criminally insane and cold-blooded killers of that ilk in the long term.

Several deaths have occurred throughout the jail's entire ninety-year history. One of them does not appear in any of the written records at all; as such, it is purely anecdotal and should therefore be taken with a grain of salt. A prisoner is said to have fallen to his death from the second-floor balcony of the men's cellblock. Assuming that this death did actually take place, whether this unfortunate inmate slipped and fell (unlikely, as a guardrail lines the balcony), was deliberately pushed by another prisoner, or simply lost the will to live and jumped, is unknown.

We are on firmer ground when it comes to the death of a female in the women's holding area and the fact that a male prisoner hanged himself on the main cellblock, as both deaths have been corroborated by the museum curator, Michelle.

Another tragic inmate was James Bacon, a former Teller County Assemblyman who fell from grace in 1913 when he was accused of murdering his wife and stepdaughter. The stove in their kitchen exploded so violently that the authorities suspected dynamite to have been the cause. Bacon was wounded and hospitalized in the aftermath of the explosion, while his wife, Ida, and her six-year-old daughter, Josephine, were killed outright. The house itself was reduced to rubble.

Once he regained consciousness, James Bacon told detectives from his hospital bed that he had received two anonymous handwritten warning notes in the weeks before the day of the explosion. The first, he claimed, simply warned, "Beware: You and your family get out of town." The second upped the ante: "Now get out you and your family; you have been notified before, if you don't you will go out on a stretcher." Additionally, Bacon said that each threat was marked with the sign of a black hand.

Despite a hefty $250 reward in exchange for help with identifying potential suspects, no information was forthcoming, and suspicion soon fell on the former assemblyman himself. Bacon was incarcerated in the Cripple Creek Jail, where he maintained his innocence and promptly went on a hunger strike, refusing to eat anything other than an orange each day.

As the days passed, James Bacon grew weaker and thinner. Periodically, he would break the fast and eat, before going back to a starvation diet once more. Finally, the prisoner slashed himself across the chest and upper belly with a knife that one of the guards had given him so that he could trim his nails. The cut was deep enough to eviscerate him, and when the guards found him the next morning, Bacon's intestines were clearly seen to be poking out through the abdominal wall. The wounded man was taken to hospital, where he subsequently died of an infection, a very common cause of death where abdominal wounds are concerned.

Even though the dying man claimed that he had been assaulted by masked men who had entered his cell in the middle of the night, the coroner ruled that Bacon's death was one of suicide. To his dying breath, James Bacon maintained his innocence. No other suspect in the death of his family was ever identified. I couldn't help but wonder exactly what had happened in his cell that night, and whether he really had been cold-blooded enough to blow up his own wife and stepdaughter.

What must James Bacon's thoughts have been when he was locked up behind these thick jail walls? Either he was falsely accused of the murders, which must have caused bitter resentment, or alternatively, he was guilty as charged and had to live his last days with the knowledge that he was responsible for taking two innocent lives. No matter which turned out to be the case (and it is unlikely that we will ever know for sure), the emotions that he felt would probably have been strong, intense, and very negative. Did anything of them still remain, I wondered, in the form of some type of psychic scar?

Theft and burglary were rife in and around the town. Stage-coach and train robberies were not uncommon, and the local merchants often had their stores cleaned out by brazen thieves. A constant stream of money and valuable goods flowed into and out of Cripple Creek along the roads and railways, which provided ample opportunities for crooks to rip them off—usually at gunpoint. Those armed robbers who didn't make a clean escape were either shot down in the process or ended up being taken alive by the lawmen and transported to the jail.

I spent almost an hour wandering the hallways and reading the many stories of life behind bars that had been collected and posted by the dedicated museum staff. Surprisingly, it wasn't all gloom and doom; one tale that brought a smile to my face took place in 1908, when an illicit wedding took place between an inmate named Hans Albert and a woman name Grace Hadsell. Despite being separated by the sturdy jail walls, the two love-birds were married by an obliging pastor. The blushing bride stood on a stack of dry goods boxes outside the jail, while her fiancé put his face to the cell bars and took her by the hand so that they might be joined in marriage. I couldn't help but admire their sheer effrontery while also feeling sympathetic for their plight; after all, there was no way that the Albert marriage was consummated on their wedding night...

Although illegal in Cripple Creek, prostitution was a fact of everyday life, and the authorities generally turned a blind eye. The gold camp had its own version of a red-light district, which conveniently segregated the so-called soiled doves and corralled them into a single area, well away from the eyes of the general populace. Despite the objection of some residents, the amount of taxable income that the prostitutes brought in was too great to be ignored, and so their presence was tolerated rather than welcomed. Nevertheless, they were still arrested and incarcerated in some cases, usually for such nebulous crimes as "sport" and the wearing of "lewd dress."

Our host Michelle informed me that the first two bookings in the jail were a pair of alleged prostitutes, both of whom were charged with assault with a deadly weapon—apparently, they had attacked a customer when he refused to pay them for their services. Having spent countless hours poring over the written documentation of the time, Michelle pointed out that at no time was the actual term *prostitution* used.

I was interested to see that there was a cellblock for males and a separate one for women, with such segregation of the sexes considered only proper for the time the jail was in operation. The women's wing was upstairs, and we were informed that one of the resident spirits was believed to be that of the original female jailer, whose proper title was *Matron*. She was responsible for overseeing the needs of the female inmates on a day-to-day basis. A compact set of living quarters can still be found up there to this day, set aside entirely for the Matron's personal use. She was said to be very particular about the way in which things were done in what was still, in her mind, her jail, and woe betide the visitor who was caught behaving with disrespect inside her section of the building.

The wooden staircase leading up to the female wing was the scene of numerous accounts of phantom footsteps, which had been heard by both staff and visitors going up or down the stairs. Whenever somebody went to check on the source of the footsteps, there was never anybody there. This sounded like an entirely residual phenomenon, the type of atmospheric recording that can somehow be imprinted upon a place over the years.

I found myself wondering just how many times the jailer had made her way up and down these creaking stairs, leading her latest charge into the cells or perhaps conveying her back downstairs for transfer to the courthouse. There is a commonly held theory among members of the paranormal research community that repetitive activity such as this can work its way into the fabric of an environment somehow—although the recording process isn't entirely understood, an analogy might be the way in which flowing water erodes channels and pathways through even the strongest rock if it is given sufficient time to do so.

The staff living quarters were clean and pleasant. Bright and airy, they would stand in stark contrast to our next stop on the walk-through: the cellblocks themselves.

The main cellblocks were built on two levels, with each level containing fourteen individual cells. As we passed each one, I took a quick look inside. They were gray, gloomy, and Spartan in appearance, just as one would expect. Our guide told us that each cell typically held up to six men, which must have been incredibly cramped and definitely less than hygienic—there was only one toilet for the entire tier of cells. In other words, the prisoners of each tier had to share a single toilet, which could only have added to the misery of everyday life on the cellblock.

As we passed one of the ground-floor cells, I suddenly got the shock of my life. There, standing in the corner and staring at me, was the figure of a man. No, not just a man—a prisoner. He was wearing white coveralls with banded black stripes and giving me a glassy-eyed stare that went straight through me. The man stood completely still, not moving a muscle.

To my credit, I managed not to scream. Only then did I realize that rather than coming face to face with an apparition, I had actually encountered a mannequin, posed there by the museum staff in order to add a little atmosphere to the proceedings. I don't know about atmosphere, but it certainly added to my heart rate! I had practically jumped out of my skin.

Continuing to look around, I was struck by the graffiti that had been etched into the walls, ceilings, and floors by countless prisoners over the years, usually scratched by some sort of sharp implement. Some of it was in the form of crude humor, as one would expect, and made me chuckle. Some was practical, such as the helpful note cut into the wall on the upper cellblock that read, "132 laps = 1 mile." That evoked images of the prisoners shuffling round and round the metal flooring high above the ground, then measuring the amount of ground they had covered by how many laps went into a mile.

A sense of despair tended to pervade the graffiti in many of the cells, such as one note that read "It dose'nt [sic] get any better than this." "Welcome to Hell!" declared the scrawl above the door to cell number 2, which was rebutted by the rather more positive "No whining!"

The cell that stands out in my mind today was practically a work of art. Whoever had lived there clearly had an artistic flair, because they had covered the interior from floor to ceiling with drawings that made it look like the inside of a house. There were hand-drawn bricks, a chimney and fireplace, and a window (complete with sketched-in prison bars) looking out on a beautifully drawn view of the Rocky Mountains with a blue lake and scattered trees in the foreground. A grandiose banner arching above the cell door proclaimed it to be "Ron's Place," although a handwritten note below declared that this had also been "Jerry's Place for 70 days." The effect was slightly spoiled by a crudely drawn swastika.

I stood inside Ron's Place for a moment, soaking up the gloomy atmosphere and thinking about the steady parade of men that had been locked away inside this place over the years. If these walls could only speak...

Some of the graffiti was downright heartbreaking. One note that simply read "I love my baby" brought a tear to my eye. So many wasted lives, so many strong emotions—few of them positive.

I am often asked why a certain place might be haunted. During the course of my more than twenty-year journey into the paranormal, I have come to believe that where one finds extremely strong and sustained emotion, one also finds ghosts. This link has arisen time and time again on case after case. In some instances, the emotions in question are happy ones, causing entities such as those who linger on in a place long after their physical death because they were particularly happy and content in their former home. The activity in these types of haunting is usually fairly benign, lacking the fear factor and sometimes outright violence that is prevalent in some of the darker cases.

Those cases can often be quite disturbing and tend to occur in places where there has been a great deal of pain, suffering, and misery over a protracted period of time. Battlefields such as Gettysburg fit the bill (more Americans died in agony over the course of three days on that bloody ground than died during the entire Vietnam War), as do some hospitals, asylums, and many prisons—all places in which the prevailing emotions are consistently negative.

Pondering this, I made my way back to the main entrance. The atmosphere inside the jail was somewhat dense and heavy. Then again, I reminded myself that this was a place of imprisonment, after all, and they are seldom places of joy and light. Added to that was the fact that the jail was reputed to be haunted, and the ghost stories had already predisposed my mind to feeling just a little creeped out. The mind is a strange thing, and it doesn't take much to fuel the imagination when one steps foot into a dark and nearly deserted old building that is said to be awash with spirits.

A Growl in the Dark

Along with seasoned investigator Aurthur McClelland, Colton had established an operations center in the gift shop. Case after case of equipment was stacked up around the edges of the room. Banks of radios were charging from power outlets. A lot of the setup work had already been done by these two men and their teammates, who had run cables to various cameras that had been strategically positioned throughout the building. Although there were a few blind spots (unavoidable in a building this large), the cameras were providing good coverage of many of the darkened hallways and cellblocks.

Even more ambitiously, Colton was live-streaming the camera feeds out to the world via the internet, allowing interested viewers to follow along with us in real time. It was fully dark outside, and after the obligatory smoke break for those who partook (and a drink of soda for those of us who didn't) we divided up into small teams, selected our equipment, and went to the locations that our leaders had selected for us. We made a point of setting our cell phones to airplane mode to make sure that they wouldn't trigger false positives on our EMF meters.

Catlyn and I started out in the female jailer's quarters upstairs. We sat there in the near-darkness for half an hour, our backs to the iron bedframe, just getting accustomed to our environment and putting ourselves in the right frame of mind for an investigation. We ran a digital voice recorder and a K2 EMF meter in the center of the room, but nothing unusual turned up. On playback, the audio contained nothing more than the passing of cars outside every few minutes.

Finally, our radio crackled to life. Colton was deploying us to a new location—the women's cellblock. Having drawn a blank in the living quarters, we settled ourselves in on the landing outside the cells. We were a little more active this time, calling out questions to the air around us in an attempt to coax any resident spirits to come forward and make their presence known to us.

Once again, nothing.

Neither of us was particularly frustrated. Contrary to what you may have seen on TV, at least ninety percent of the time spent on a paranormal investigation is fruitless. We spent a lot of time sitting around in the dark hoping that something anomalous will happen, but the vast majority of that time passes slowly and peacefully.

The remaining ten percent makes it all worth it.

"Nothing happening here," Catlyn reported into the walkie-talkie when Colton checked in with us.

The main cellblock at Cripple Creek,
scene of countless years' worth of misery and anger.

"Come on down for a break," he instructed. We made our way slowly down the steep staircase, being extra cautious in the darkness. I cracked open the night's second can of Mountain Dew and enjoyed another caffeine bolus. Aurthur and Colton were keeping a watchful eye on the monitors, providing a commentary for the online viewers. Things were still pretty quiet inside the old jail, but they weren't going to stay that way for long.

For the next round of investigation, Colton wanted to get his hands dirty. He went down to the basement along with Matt Laughlin, one of his colleagues. I had scoped the basement out earlier; it was full of cleaning supplies and massive stacks of leather-bound antique books, which turned out to be volumes of Colorado statutes and case law, and a beautiful horse-drawn carriage. There were also fluorescent strip lights and a great deal of electrical wiring running along the underside of the ceiling, all potential power sources that entities might use as a fuel source in order to manifest—and manifest they most certainly would, as Colton and Matt were about to find out.

The two men were conducting an EVP session, sitting side by side on a bench. A digital voice recorder was running in an adjacent room, capturing every word they spoke. Things were proceeding smoothly and quietly at the beginning, but the investigators persisted in calmly asking questions, hoping that responses would turn up on the recordings once they were played back during the evidence review phase.

The growl took them both by surprise, harsh and guttural.

"What the f— was that?" Colton said.

Their heads whipped around to the left. Colton and Matt peered into the shadows of the adjoining room, certain that they were looking in the direction that the disturbing sound had originated from. They were absolutely sure that the room was empty; it had been checked before they sat down to begin their session, and the entrances and exits were covered by the remote cameras. If a flesh-and-blood human being had been responsible, they would have been caught in the act.

Nevertheless, Colton went through to check the room out thoroughly. It was completely empty, as it had been all along. The investigators went to retrieve their digital voice recorder, which they had unfortunately positioned in a different room. They half-suspected that the device was too far away to pick up the growl, but when they played the recording back, they were elated to find that the throaty rumble had indeed been recorded for posterity; on playback, it was absolutely loud and clear.

Frankly, the sound gave me the chills.

As we huddled around the voice recorder in the operations center while Colton played the ten-second track over and over again, opinion was divided on what the sound actually was. Most of those present thought that it was a disembodied growl, but my opinion was that it could have been the noise of somebody getting their throat cut. It was a messy, glottal kind of sound.

"Perhaps it's the sound of somebody hacking up a lung," I suggested, setting my throat-cutting theory aside. As a paramedic, I had heard many patients whose lungs were filled with fluid and mucus. The wet cough of somebody trying desperately to clear their lower airway was something you never forgot, and the anomalous recording reminded me of some of those patients. Historically, respiratory infections would have run rampant in a place such as this, where inmates were packed in like sardines, living on top of one another, coughing and sneezing into one another's airspace. Diseases such as tuberculosis would have spread like wildfire.

Although we weren't exactly sure of what Colton's recorder had actually captured, one thing we could all agree upon was that this was no ordinary EVP. Typically, electronic voice phenomena are not heard with the human ear at the time of recording, showing up only on playback; even then, most such phenomena can be very hard to hear, requiring headphones and a little cleanup with audio enhancement software. This recording, on the other hand, was both loud and crystal clear, and the growl had been heard by both of the witnesses at the time it took place.

To this day, I'm still not sure precisely what it was that Colton and his colleague captured in the basement of the Cripple Creek Jail, but it stands as one of the most impressive pieces of audio evidence that I have ever heard. I can think of no rational, non-paranormal explanation for the sound, and at the time of writing it remains unexplained.

Locked Down

Things were gathering steam, and we had no idea that this was only the beginning. This crucial piece of evidence did wonders for our morale, putting an extra spring into our step. Our next stop was the main cellblock, where we intended to try a little stimulation. Each of us selected a cell of our own. I picked one in the middle of the block and sat down on the floor, settling my back against the cold wall.

When the lights went down, one of the investigators began to walk the block, running a stick along the metal bars in such a way that it made my teeth clench. This guy was big, solidly built, and a great fit for the role of prison guard, which he now began to portray with relish. Our jailer continued to walk the beat, calling out to us in the darkness, asserting his authority and taunting the inmates who were trapped in his cells.

I like to think of myself as being a fairly imaginative sort of person, and it was no effort at all for me to put myself in the shoes of one of those convicts, trapped behind bars and unable to get out. Having spent fifteen years as a firefighter, I have learned that claustrophobia is most definitely something that I do not suffer from, yet even I could feel that the prison walls seemed to be closing in on me from all sides. No matter what they had done wrong, I was starting to develop empathy for those unfortunate souls who had been incarcerated here.

We were only locked down on that cellblock for half an hour, but it felt like an eternity. Our "guard" had played his part to perfection, and I was all too happy when it was time to make our way back for another break. This time, I went outside with the smokers and enjoyed the cool night air for a while. Chatting back and forth, most of us felt that the energies inside the prison were building, perhaps because there were so many investigators present that night.

"So where do you want to go next?" Colton asked. I had no hesitation in replying.

"The cellblock upstairs, if that's all right." Some of the other investigators had reported getting some interesting activity up there, the sound of footsteps and whispered voices. I had been tempted to dismiss both things as coming from those of us who were downstairs on the main cellblock; after all, sound carries, particularly at night, and the acoustics of old buildings can sometimes be rather strange. I would soon be shown the error of my ways.

Catlyn and I climbed the staircase to the uppermost floor, following the walkway around and selecting one of the cells at random. After calling in on the radio to report that we were in place, we waited for our fellow investigators to find their own positions before beginning our investigation.

At first, things were quiet and peaceful. That changed quickly, however. Catlyn and I looked at one another at about the same time. "Can you hear that?" we both asked.

"Voices," Catlyn said, and I nodded in agreement. Each of us was hearing the same thing. On comparing notes, we concurred that it sounded as if snatches of conversation were coming from somewhere out of the darkness.

Thinking that it might be our fellow investigators down on the main cellblock exercising poor noise discipline, I called out to them through the cell door and politely asked them to keep the noise down.

"Nobody's talking down here!" one of them hollered back.

The cell walls were extremely thick and solid, which should have acted as a dampener for many of the stray sounds, but the voices were coming thicker and faster, growing in both intensity and frequency. Neither of us seriously believed that they could be originating from the floor below us any longer. They seemed to be coming from out of thin air all around us.

If you have ever stayed in a hotel room and listened to a party going on downstairs or in the room next door, then you have experienced something similar to what we were hearing that night: the sound of multiple voices, all of them just on the edge of hearing, speaking unintelligibly but with great gusto.

"Can you make out what they're saying?" I asked Catlyn, the frustration apparent in my tone. She shook her head. We were hearing what I can only describe as a constant background whispering or muttering. No matter how much we strained our ears, we were unable to interpret any of the words, though I was convinced that we were listening to multiple speakers going back and forth. All I could do was hope that the audio recorder was picking it up, which would allow me to amplify the voices with computer software in an attempt to make them clearer.

The voices died off after a few minutes, and silence returned to the upper cellblock once more. I took a seat in one corner, while Catlyn stood inside the entrance. All that I could see in the dimness was her slim silhouette blotting out what little ambient light was trying to get into the cell through the doorway. Standing there impassively with her head cocked to one side, just listening, she reminded me of a prison guard standing watch over an inmate.

Doppelgänger

After a few minutes, I heard the distinctive sound of footsteps approaching us along the balcony outside the cell. Turning, Catlyn offered a cheery hello to Shaun Crusha, one of our fellow investigators for the evening. He was very kindly coming to see how we were getting along. Stepping aside, Catlyn made room for Shaun to come into the cell. When he saw me sitting there in the corner, the seasoned paranormal investigator stopped dead in his tracks, his jaw dropping open in apparent disbelief.

"How did you get back inside so fast?" he demanded, staring at me with a very strange expression on his face. When I told Shaun that I had absolutely no idea what he was talking about, he went on to explain that he had just seen me standing on the upper cellblock close to the top of the stairs. How on earth had I managed to slip past him and sneak back into this cell before he entered it?

Catlyn explained that I had been here all along and that Shaun could not possibly have encountered me outside on the balcony, but Shaun stuck to his guns. As a long-serving veteran of the US Air Force and a man with an extensive background in paranormal research, he was not one to be easily fooled. Bringing out a flashlight, Shaun looked around the cell and satisfied himself that there were no other ways in or out.

"It was you, Richard. I recognized your face. You were standing there just looking up, as though you were going to take photos."

He went on to describe what I was beginning to think was my doppelgänger. According to German folklore, this is a sort of evil twin, a perfect imitation of a living human being. The concept is not unique to Germanic society, however—many cultures around the world have their equivalent versions. The legends say that if somebody encounters their own doppelgänger, they are doomed to die sometime in the very near future. My flesh broke out in goosebumps at the mere thought of it.

Had Shaun really encountered something at the top of that staircase that looked exactly like me? When Catlyn and I questioned him further, Shaun confirmed that the version of me that he had encountered outside the cell had exactly the same face and hair that I did and was also dressed almost identically to me … almost, but not quite. The shirt color was different.

This raised some intriguing possibilities. Had there been a time-slip, one in which I returned to the Cripple Creek Jail at a future date and was dressed slightly differently? Or was one of the resident entities masquerading as me, wearing my face and very similar clothing but not quite getting an exact match? Whatever the explanation was, the concepts were all a little chilling.

Shaun hadn't thought to take a photograph of the figure. After all, why should he? Until he had entered my jail cell, he had quite naturally assumed that the man he had encountered at the top of the staircase was the flesh-and-blood Richard Estep. The apparition had appeared completely solid, lacking even the slightest hint of transparency or otherworldliness. I wondered what would have happened if Shaun had reached out and touched it. Would he have laid his hand on warm skin, or would his fingertips have passed through the thing's body as if it weren't really there?

This wasn't the first time in my life that I had been gifted with a paranormal imitator of some sort. When investigating a reputedly very haunted sanatorium in the south, two investigators claimed to have heard my voice speaking loudly from the underground body chute, a long, steep tunnel used for the transportation of corpses. The catch was that I was up on the roof at the time, many feet above them and at the other end of the building.

There was also the case of the old Tooele Valley Hospital outside Salt Lake City in Utah, now known by the more frightening moniker of Asylum 49. I had been sitting in the operations center watching over my teammates on the security cameras when one of them had excitedly called me out into the hallway. The team had been conducting a spirit box session, attempting to get the spirits of the former hospital to communicate with them via a radio frequency scanner, when all of a sudden the box began to call out my name in a voice that sounded distinctly British in character. Some of those present felt that they were actually hearing my voice emanating from the speaker, which was of course an absolute impossibility.

My home for the evening,
a cell in the old Cripple Creek Jail.

Now my phantom twin had put in an appearance. What, if anything, did it all mean?

Still discussing the ramifications, the three of us returned to join our colleagues in the operations center. Everyone had an opinion on what had happened, and we hoped that the cameras had captured the spectral intruder on film; but when Aurthur and Colton replayed the footage, we were all greatly disappointed to find that the camera lens wasn't quite covering that section of the upper balcony. Whatever had taken place, it had happened in one of the many blind spots in our CCTV network.

The whispering voices quieted down after that, and it seemed as though energy levels were dropping. With dawn not too far away, we decided to call it a night and began the long and laborious process of breaking down and packing away our equipment.

To this day, Shaun remains adamant about what he saw that night. The details and particulars of his testimony have not changed one iota, and he remains every bit as puzzled about the incident as I am. I am not sure what he encountered that night, and I feel somewhat unnerved that whatever it was, it had chosen to ape my appearance, with the minor exception of my shirt. Whether this was a spirit, time-slip, dimensional crossover, or something stranger than all that, I cannot say for sure.

I just wonder whether any other visitors to the Cripple Creek Jail have found somebody who looks just like me staring down at them when they climb the staircase to the upper cellblock.

They can rest assured that it isn't really me.

CHAPTER 2

HOSTEL WORK ENVIRONMENT

IS THIS BRITAIN'S MOST HAUNTED HOUSE? screamed a 2016 headline in the *Daily Mail*, one of the UK's most popular tabloid newspapers. POLICE SEARCHED FOR "EVIL FORCES" LOCATED IN THE SEVEN BEDROOM PROPERTY AFTER "CHILDREN'S SHADOWS AND MOVING KNIVES" ARE RE-PORTED.

When a link to the online article appeared in my email in-box, I eagerly skimmed through to the end. According to the author, no tenant had been found who was willing to stay in the house for more than a few days (the current record was four) due to the intensity of the paranormal activity.

The location in question was being touted as the most haunted house in the entire city of Hull: the house at 39 De Grey Street, more commonly known as "the Hostel."

The article went on to claim that one of the property's former residents was dragged out of bed by an invisible entity and choked, which had prompted her to call in the police. Less than impressed with the distressed homeowner's story, the responding police officers proceeded to give her a dressing-down… which ended with a bookcase falling on one of them, and a speedy exit on the part of the boys in blue.

The current owner claimed that he had encountered the shadowy apparition of a young girl, which emerged from the fireplace and remained there in plain sight for a good fifteen minutes while he watched in terror, before finally returning to disappear back into the fireplace again.

Visiting psychics reported the presence of an aggressive male entity in one of the back bedrooms, who had a penchant for growling at those who got too close.

More newspapers and websites started picking up on the story. The *Sun*, a national tabloid newspaper, sent a reporter along to spend a night in the house. In his article titled WHERE "DERANGED SPIRITS OF CHILDREN" PLAY: WE TAKE A LOOK AT THE MOST HAUNTED HOUSE IN BRITAIN, journalist Lee Price wrote of the adventure he and his cameraman say they had. This particular extract from the article made me sit bolt upright in my chair: "Not much is known about the history of the property, but various mediums and clairvoyants have pointed to a host of child spirits roaming around. They believe the children were brought here to be cared for when terminally ill, then tortured, raped and killed."

Things seemed to have begun innocuously enough (camera malfunctions and battery drains) but the overnight visit soon picked up speed, and when the flustered reporter confessed to "having had enough" and wanting to leave at 4 a.m., he claimed to have caught sight of a young boy waving goodbye to him from the attic window. Was this merely a piece of sensationalist embellishment on the part of the reporter, I wondered, or did he genuinely see the apparition of a child?

I decided to write and ask him.

"I'm really sorry, but I have no/very little recollection of my stay there," he responded to my question about the young boy, "certainly not enough to confidently be quoted on the subject. Apologies, but do feel free to quote the article."

To my mind, such incredible claims were just begging for an in-depth investigation. I subsequently made inquiries, and the owner was kind enough to offer me the run of the place for five full days and nights.

My brain kept turning the claims over and over, examining them from every angle. As a paranormal investigator, I was always up for a challenge. If no tenant could truly stand living in the Hostel for more than four days, then how was I going to fare over the course of five?

I contacted British Airways that same day and made arrangements to fly out as soon as I could in the new year.

A Contradictory History

My flight from Denver landed at London's bustling Heathrow airport just before ten o'clock on an unseasonably bright and sunny Saturday morning at the end of January. Along with fellow paranormal investigator Lesley, I made the three-hour drive

north to Kingston upon Hull, quietly appreciating the sight of
the British landscape as it went past the car windows.

Family reunion, Estep style:
my brother Matthew visits me at the Hostel.

It felt good to be home again, not only because of the chance to catch up with friends and family, but also because the opportunity beckoned for me to try and get to the bottom of another potential haunting. I had also spent a large part of my childhood in Hull, spending weekends at my grandparents' haunted house in Orchard Park, and it was amazing to see just how much the city had changed with time.

As Lesley and I checked into our hotel rooms, the receptionist politely inquired about my reasons for visiting from America. When I mentioned the property at 39 De Grey Street, an older man suddenly pricked up his ears and told us that he knew of the place and its reputation as a haunted house.

"Did you read about it on the internet or in the newspapers?" I asked. He shook his head.

"No, son. I've lived 'round here for fifty years. Known about that house for at least the last twenty-five."

That struck me as being rather interesting. In this day and age, cases of alleged hauntings can go viral in the space of just twenty-four hours, as the news-starved media outlets all pick up the same story and run with it. But if this man had first heard about the Hostel back in 1995 or so, then the news would have traveled by word of mouth and perhaps articles in the smaller local presses (and I couldn't find any of those when I checked).

We arranged to meet owner Andy Yates at the Hostel after dinner that afternoon. It was dark by the time we walked down De Grey Street, carrying bags full of equipment and a Ouija board that had once belonged to my wife's grandmother.

Andy greeted us warmly and apologized for the multiple padlocks that had to be opened before we could get inside.

There had been break-ins at one time, he explained, and so he had been forced to become more security-conscious. When I walked around the building to perform a 360-degree appraisal, I realized that he wasn't kidding. The property was completely surrounded by a high wall, on top of which were affixed coils of barbed wire. A dark and narrow alleyway ran along the left side, separating it from the building next door. When we ventured along it, I also noticed that above my head, a metal bridge connected Number 39 to its neighbor on the left side.

"Aye, that," Andy said in a broad Yorkshire accent. "Hull was bombed very heavily by the Luftwaffe during World War II. Apparently, that building next door was an undertaker's establishment. I've been told that the Hostel was used as a temporary overflow mortuary when there were a lot of deaths. Bodies used to be kept in the back and then transferred across for the morticians to work on when they were ready to prepare them for burial."

If that was indeed the case, then it might be a possible explanation for the paranormal activity that people were reporting. "Then again," I thought out loud, "that would have been more than seventy years ago."

Hull-based historian Mike Covell has spent a great deal of time researching the history of 39 De Grey Street, and his findings make for fascinating reading.

After searching the archives at the Hull History Centre, Mike found no evidence whatsoever of the house ever having been used to store bodies, nor was there any record of Number 39 or any other house on De Grey Street having been an orphanage, despite a blizzard of rumors to the contrary.

A furniture remover named John Hardaker was listed as having owned the house in the late nineteenth and early twentieth centuries, according to Mike's findings, but otherwise the house seems to have been a private residence for most of its life. Despite the chilling stories surrounding the house, he could find no references to there ever having been murders or suicides in the house either.

Mike's historical legwork may have blown away some of the more prominent claims about 39 De Grey Street's past, but that didn't necessarily mean that it wasn't haunted.

Andy led us into the kitchen and invited us on a quick tour of the place in order to get our bearings. Sadly, the building had obviously seen better days. Many of the ceilings and walls were badly water-damaged, with some of the flooring having rotted away. Andy had done what repairs he could, but the elements had still taken their toll on the structure over the years. Icy drafts whistled through the rooms and corridors, in large part due to the fact that some of the windows at the rear of the structure no longer had glass in them. That would make the monitoring of potentially paranormal cold spots almost impossible.

I had investigated a number of austere environments before, including antiquated old ruins and houses that were still under construction, but the Hostel was one of the most uncomfortable by far. There was an ever-present bone-chilling cold, and although there were two portable electric heaters upstairs and two more downstairs, it was going to be necessary for us all to stay bundled up in heavy winter clothing in order to spend our nights there.

It was raining heavily on the night of our arrival and would continue to do so for the entire week of our stay. The roof leaked, sending rainwater running down all the way from the attic to the ground floor. Everything we did was accompanied by an incessant *drip-drip-drip*, which corrupted almost all of the audio data that we would gather during our investigation.

The Girl in the Fireplace

When Andy and I stepped out into the hallway, I was surprised to see four bolts on the inside of the heavy wooden front door. The original lock had been ripped away somehow, leaving a mess of bare wood in its place.

"What happened here?" I asked, intrigued.

Andy had last lived in the house some ten years before our visit, and he said that nobody had lived at Number 39 De Grey Street for the past few years. He told me that one night several months before, a neighbor had happened to look up at one of the front windows. Staring back down at them forlornly was a little girl, perhaps seven or eight years old. The neighbor was understandably perturbed by the fact that she appeared to be trapped inside an empty house that appeared for all intents and purposes locked up and abandoned. No wonder they called 999.

When the police arrived and heard the story, they battered in the front door of Number 39, tearing the lock away in the process. After searching the seven-bedroom house from top to bottom, they found … nothing. No little girl. All other entrances to the house were locked up tight.

The four sliding bolts were the work of an emergency locksmith, who had been called out at an ungodly hour of the morning to attempt to secure the broken front door.

"The article I read mentioned you seeing the shadowy figure of a young girl," I said to Andy. He went on to tell me the full story.

One night, when he had been lying asleep in the master bedroom at the front of the house, Andy had suddenly awoken with a start. Standing there in front of the fireplace was the figure of a little girl, some seven or eight years of age. She was simply staring at him. He described her as having shoulder-length hair and a look on her face that seemed to be begging for help. After fifteen to twenty minutes, Andy was compelled to move ... and when he did, the girl disappeared back into the fireplace.

"Did she make eye contact with you?" I asked eagerly, trying to determine whether this was a residual apparition (a natural recording, much like the image on a TV screen) or an intelligent one, which should theoretically be capable of interacting with him. Those apparitions that are seen to make eye contact with the living and sometimes even speak to them often seem to want to fulfill some kind of purpose.

One of the first recorded instances of such a ghost comes to us from the era of the ancient Romans by way of Pliny the Younger, who tells of a house in Athens that was reputed to be haunted. Athenian citizens made a point of avoiding the place, and the residents finally fled, citing their terror of the apparition of a stick-thin old man who would appear each night, rattling the chains that bound his wrists and ankles.

Being a haunted house was such a stigma that nobody wanted to live there, no matter how much its increasingly desperate owner dropped the price. Finally, a philosopher named Athenodorus Cananites came to town. Seeing the ridiculously low asking price, he made inquiries and was told of the haunting by locals. Dismissing the fears of those who warned him not to do it, Athenodorus purchased the home at a bargain price and duly settled in for his first night in residence at his new villa.

Not long after dark, the rattling of chains announced the arrival of the old man's ghost, which stood in front of Athenodorus and beckoned him impatiently, demanding that the philosopher follow it. He found it easy enough to keep up, thanks to the heavy chains that bound the apparition, and when it reached a specific part of the yard, the ghost disappeared into thin air.

When slaves were ordered to dig up that part of the yard the following day at Athenodorus's direction, they uncovered the skeletal remains of a man ... one who had been bound with heavy iron chains. A dignified burial service was soon conducted, and once the old man's bones had been laid to rest, Pliny tells us that the villa was never bothered by the apparition again.

The literature of ghost lore is full of such stories: spirits that return or remain earthbound because of "unfinished business," such as murder victims whose bodies have not been given a proper interment or whose killers have not been brought to justice. If children genuinely were "tortured, raped and killed" at 39 De Grey Street (something that my research has been unable to find any evidence to support), then the apparitions of the children that have been reported there might be trying to draw attention to the ill-treatment they suffered at the hands of adults.

"Yes, she made eye contact," Andy nodded. "We stared at each other. I couldn't move. Then she backed slowly toward the fireplace and disappeared into it." He went on to tell me that three mediums, none of whom knew one another or had been to the Hostel before, had all claimed that the skeletal remains of a child were interred on the property somewhere, and one had pinpointed the chimney itself as a possible place for them to have been bricked up. Andy wasn't willing to start tearing the chimney or its surroundings apart, for obvious reasons, but he had found the claims to be somewhat unnerving to say the least.

Meet Stephen

Cold, damp, and jet-lagged, I nevertheless wanted to get straight down to the business of investigating. Luckily for me, a trusted old friend and comrade had agreed to come and join us for the night. Gaynor Clarke had been the corporal who had taught me the art of military radio communications during our time in the Territorial Army some twenty years before. Corporal Clarke had gone on to become Sergeant Clarke and served during the wars in the Middle East, whereas Private Estep had packed up and moved to the USA in order to start a new life, so our paths had diverged significantly since the last time we had seen each other. It was wonderful to catch up over a cup of hot tea (thank you, Lesley!). When Gaynor had heard that I would be investigating at De Grey Street, she had volunteered her time and expertise. Although she knew next to nothing about paranormal investigation, her military skill set and temperament made her ideally suited for the job, and I was only too happy to have her along.

Sitting in the master bedroom, we began an EVP session. It was so bitterly cold that we had to gather around an electric heater in order to prevent our teeth from chattering. A voice came from close to the fireplace from which Andy said he had seen the spirit of the girl emerge: "That tickles!" the voice giggled.

This was our extra investigator, a teddy bear that went by the name of Stephen. He was no ordinary bear. Stephen was a commercially made ghost-hunting tool called a "Boo Buddy" that was a combination EMF meter, vibration sensor, and thermometer, all wrapped up in a package designed to entice the spirits of children to come out and play with him. If something attempted to touch, hug, squeeze, or move any part of his tiny frame, the Boo Buddy wouldn't be shy about letting me know. Stephen was also programmed to speak, uttering lines from children's nursery rhymes and games. I had used him with some success when investigating Denver's haunted Botanic Gardens, and after rechristening him Stephen (after my favorite ghost-hunting priest), I had brought him across the Atlantic to help me investigate the Hostel.

When Stephen claimed that he was being tickled, the sensors were detecting motion. Something was moving the teddy bear, yet as we all turned to look at it, we could not see any possible cause for it. Outside the boarded-up windows, De Grey Street was quiet, with no passing traffic to send vibrations up into the building's structure.

"Brrrr—it's cold in here!" Now Stephen was indicating a localized temperature drop. Admittedly, the room was extremely cold, but with an electric heater turned up to its maximum output and the additional body warmth of three people, the air temperature shouldn't have been going down. The reverse should have been true.

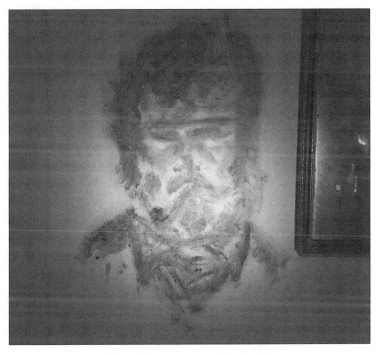

*The dark male entity that is said
to hold the Hostel in the grip of fear.*

When we repeated the experiment in child's bedroom next door, the temperature remained consistent, but a child's rocking horse began to rock back and forth by itself. The movement wasn't spectacular, and again I found myself wondering whether vibrations from somewhere were running through the structure and causing the slight movement, which wasn't forceful enough for me to call paranormal.

Interesting, but hardly spectacular, which really summed up the entire night. After sleeping the following morning and afternoon away, we saw Gaynor off and welcomed our friend Nat Wilson, an experienced paranormal investigator of many years' standing who also runs one of the UK's largest paranormal tour companies. She had long been fascinated with the stories surrounding the Hostel and had jumped at my offer to come along and experience the place for herself.

We started off in the front room. With the windows boarded up, the only light that entered was that which filtered through from the dining room. When I played my flashlight beam around, the image of a man's head and shoulders stared down at us from one of the bare walls. It had been daubed in what appeared to be grease (see page 43). According to Andy, it had suddenly appeared one night after a paranormal research team had visited. The visitors all denied being responsible for what was basically an act of vandalism. I couldn't help but wonder if this was a representation of one of the spirits that was said to haunt the place.

Adventures in Ouija

We started with a Ouija session. I had brought a board along with me from the United States. It had belonged to the late grandmother of my wife, Laura, and Laura had asked her to keep a watchful eye over the board during our stay in De Grey Street, with an emphasis on keeping me safe from any unsavory characters that might try to come through. This was the board we set out to use first of all, huddling around it in the light of two flickering candles. I was wearing fingerless gloves to stave off the cold and lightly rested my fingertips on the planchette before opening up the board to only positive entities that wished to communicate.

Unfortunately, try as we might, the planchette refused to budge. The three of us swept it around the board in an attempt to infuse it with a little energy, but the pointer obstinately stayed still.

After a wasted quarter of an hour, Lesley suggested that we go to plan B: there was a spirit board already in the house, courtesy of a previous visitor. This wasn't a commercial board, as mine was; the words, letters, and numbers had been hand-painted on top of a flimsy wooden table. We had found it in an upstairs bedroom and brought it down to act as a backup.

The difference between the new board and the old one was like that between night and day. No sooner had we opened it up than the planchette began to fly between the letters. Whatever we were communicating with seemed to prefer yes-no answers and flatly refused to give anything in the way of details where its identity was concerned other than its age (seventy-three) and gender (male). Although it appeared that we might be making progress, something about the responses struck all three of us as being questionable. The invisible communicator went on to claim that it was by turns a seven-year-old girl and a thirty-something-year-old man. While it might be possible that multiple entities were competing for control of the spirit board, I thought it equally likely that we were dealing with a trickster entity that sought to mislead us and waste our time for its own nefarious purposes. This is a fairly common occurrence where spirit boards are concerned, and although we had specifically expressed our intention to work with only good-natured entities, it was still a very real possibility in a location that was as haunted as the Hostel was purported to be.

The fact that my wife had asked her grandmother to keep an eye on both myself and the board also wasn't lost on me. Could her protective influence possibly be the reason for my personal Ouija board not working?

As the planchette swept back and forth across the board, the answers it gave became increasingly nonsensical and inconsistent. My suspicions that we were being taken for fools began to grow, and when I flat-out asked about it, the invisible communicator admitted that yes, we were being toyed with. Annoyed, I ended the Ouija session and closed down the board appropriately, firmly stating our willingness to work with only honest and truthful spirits.

A loud screech sounded from somewhere outside the room, giving all of us quite a start. We looked up from the board. It was the REM Pod, which had been carefully sited at the top of the staircase. The REM Pod generates its own field of electromagnetic energy, which some people believe spirit entities are sometimes able to manipulate or distort in some way, either deliberately or unintentionally. While this is no more than a theory, it is an intriguing one, and many paranormal investigators have reported fascinating anomalous results when using the device. The device had been quiet all night up until now but was suddenly detecting a strong electromagnetic field from somewhere.

Nat, Lesley, and I had taken up position in the mirror room upstairs, so called because it was adorned with full-length mirrors propped against all four walls. Some visitors had attempted to use the room for the purpose of scrying. We were starting out with a

Ouija board session. No sooner had we started than EMF spikes began to register on our meters. By itself, this was puzzling; we had been diligent about switching off our personal cell phones at the beginning of the night for just this very reason. Whatever was generating an electromagnetic field, it wasn't something that we had brought into the house with us.

The session itself was going poorly. Neither of the Ouija boards that were being used seemed to want to cooperate, the planchette remaining stubbornly still.

Boom!

Startled, we all looked up from the board. A single loud knock came from somewhere in the main hallway.

"Somebody just hit the front door," Nat said. I was up and moving straight away, taking the stairs two at a time. It took a moment for me to unlock the four bolts that secured the front door. When I swung it open, there was nobody outside. Stepping out into the street, I saw a figure disappearing around the corner at the end of the road.

The most obvious explanation would be that we had just been pranked by a passerby, probably a local resident who had noticed that the hallway light was switched on and had decided to try and give us a scare. Fortunately, we didn't have to guess; Andy had installed external CCTV cameras for added security, and one of them was mounted to the outside wall facing the street. Its field of vision included the front door. I made a note of the time (10:54 p.m.) and vowed to ask Andy to check the video feed when he came back the following evening.

A tea break beckoned, giving Nat and Lesley the chance to pop outside into the street in order to smoke. Ten minutes later we were investigating again, this time focusing our attention on the staircase itself. At the top of the stairs, our REM Pod was going berserk, constantly alarming to indicate the presence of a strong electromagnetic field. It had behaved like this earlier in the night, and we had been unable to figure out exactly why back then. But on closer inspection, we found some electrical wiring behind a panel in the wall. Another mystery solved: this was no ghost.

Using our handheld EMF meters, we located the farthest edge of the EMF field and placed the REM Pod well out of its range, which meant positioning it at the edge of the top step. It stayed quiet now that there was no electrical current to trigger it.

Relocating ourselves to the master bedroom, we opened up another Ouija session and invited only positive entities to make contact with us. The steady background *drip-drip-drip* of rainwater leaking through the roof accompanied Nat's opening up of the board as a means of communication. A candle flickered next to the board to add a bit of ambience (and, if I'm honest, even a tiny fraction of extra heat was to be welcomed).

We took turns asking the standard questions. The planchette obstinately refused to move. After no more than a few minutes, I heard Lesley's breathing pattern change subtly. I looked up at her and saw that she was staring sightlessly off into the darkness, her eyes glassy and unblinking. Nudging Nat gently with my elbow, I nodded toward Lesley.

"Are you all right?" I asked. Lesley didn't answer. "What's up? Lesley? Lesley?"

"Can you talk?" Nat asked, obviously concerned. "Do you know where you are?"

Still Lesley didn't answer. Her face was an impassive mask, the only movement in it being the candlelight reflecting from her eyes.

"Aaaah!" she suddenly gasped, in the manner of somebody who had been holding their breath for a long time. When Nat and I asked her what had happened, she replied that she did not know. Her mind had gone completely blank for almost a minute. "What happened? What was I doing?"

We explained that she had been unresponsive to us, seemingly in her own little world and ignoring everything that Nat and I were saying. She had reminded me strongly of the medical patients I had seen who were suffering from absence seizures, episodes of blankness in which uncoordinated electrical activity is firing inside the brain. The classic presentation of an absence seizure is the person in which "the lights are on, but nobody's at home," meaning that the eyes are open, but the sufferer is not reacting to stimuli in the outside world. That description fit Lesley's episode of strange behavior perfectly, yet when I asked her about it, she told me firmly that she had never been diagnosed with absence seizures in her entire life. I also knew that absence seizures are far more common in children than they are in adults and rarely manifest so late in life.

Nat asked any spirits present if they were responsible for what had just happened and requested that they try to influence her or me in the same way. Now the planchette began to move, although the motion was painfully weak and slow at first. It indicated that the entity communicating through it was a male, and not a child. It claimed to have moved into 39 De Grey Street in 1924 and lived there for twelve years.

"Did you die in this house?" I asked. The planchette moved very quickly toward YES.

"Did you die in 1936?" added Nat, garnering another YES. She got the same answer when asking whether the spirit was happy here, something that we found very encouraging. Nat suddenly experienced a sense of extreme cold around her feet and lower legs, although mine, which were about six inches away from hers, felt no colder than they had all along.

Unfortunately, when the messages progressed beyond yes-no or numeric answers, they descended into absolute gibberish, so we went back to the more basic method. We were told that two more entities were present and that two of them were children who were being kept here against their will (in each case, this was a very strong YES). The board communicator denied being the one responsible for holding the children captive.

We were told that the children were not downstairs, but rather that they were located in the fireplace. I asked whether the human remains of a child were hidden in the chimney somewhere and also received a strong YES. After asking a clarifying question, the board claimed that it was the body of a little girl. For once, I found myself actively hoping that we really weren't communicating with spirits, as it would have meant that at least one child had met a grisly fate somewhere in this house. Hopefully, this was all a product of our collective subconscious...

A high-pitched screeching took us all by surprise. It was the REM Pod again, going absolutely berserk at the top of the stairs. Nat charged off to investigate. I was right behind her, with Lesley watching both our backs. The alarm was constant and extremely loud, indicating that a very high level of energy was present. We had switched off all but one of the lights in the building, so the house wiring should have been carrying less of an electrical load, not more.

We conducted a few more EVP sessions throughout the house, hitting all the remaining upstairs bedrooms. During one of the sessions, Nat remarked that her left hand had just gone cold. While interesting in itself, it hardly constituted evidence—making people cold was something that the Hostel excelled at, especially in January. It was only when I was reviewing the audio files during the evidence review phase that I realized there had been more going on than met the eye, because just a few seconds after Nat had spoken, the sound of what I can only describe as either a cat meowing or a baby crying is heard, coming from right there in the room with us... twice.

Needless to say, there were no cats or babies with us in the Hostel that night, and while there were some pigeons nesting in the garage, this was most definitely not the noise that a pigeon makes. Over our five nights at 39 De Grey Street, we heard the pigeons on several occasions, and they always sounded much different from the noise that turned up on the recording.

An Unexpected Visitor

The following evening, after Lesley and I waved Nat off and after a few hours' sleep, we eagerly awaited the arrival of Andy. We wanted to know if his CCTV cameras could shed some light on our mysterious door knocker.

Winding the security footage back to 10:54 p.m. the previous day, we peered intently at the computer monitor. My heart sank when I saw a hooded figure walk up to the front door at

10:53, pound on it with his fist, and then saunter casually away toward the far end of the street.

"Well, there goes our so-called ghost," I grumbled. "Somebody on their way back from the pub. Case closed."

Except that it wasn't, not quite. About an hour after we had checked the security camera, the three of us were chatting in the living room when another series of blows thudded on the front door. There were three this time, but they were equally loud and forceful. Once again, when Andy and I went out into the street to check, we couldn't see the culprit. We checked the side alley and looked behind all of the possible areas of concealment that we could find, but still drew a blank.

"Let's check the camera to see where the little bugger went," Andy suggested. I was admittedly less than enthusiastic at the idea, reasoning that it was the same would-be comedian from the night before, but agreed to take a look. This time, however, things were different. We wound the footage back to the time of the blows and then a further ten minutes, just to be sure. The tiny front yard of the Hostel was empty and silent. The time of the thudding came and went. Nobody was visible on the camera. No hand was seen hitting the front door, which then opened to let me and Andy out into the street.

"Unless our friend from last night has got Harry Potter's invisibility cloak, then I have no idea what just happened," I was forced to admit, genuinely perplexed. There was no way that somebody could have approached the front door and hit it repeatedly without the camera picking them up...and yet the CCTV camera proved beyond all shadow of a doubt that there had been nobody standing outside at the time.

Choked

Our next set of visitors came from a group I had met while investigating another case. My friends from East Drive Paranormal sent a detachment of investigators to assist Lesley and me at the Hostel. The rain was torrential when their cars parked outside the house, which had both its good and bad points. On the one hand, the constant drumming of raindrops both outside and coming in through the leaky roof would play havoc with our audio data, but on the other, there are several theories floating around that storms tend to heighten paranormal activity due to some natural mechanism that we don't yet understand. I hoped that really would turn out to be the case.

Our team for the night would be Carol, Claire, Eileen, Kayla, Jason, Angie, and owner Andy Yates, plus Lesley and myself. It was to be our last night at the Hostel and I was hoping for a grand finale.

Carol and Jason both claimed to have psychic abilities (I cannot say either way because I have never put either of them to the test), and I was looking forward to seeing what they might pick up on at 39 De Grey Street, a building that they had never stepped foot inside until now.

It didn't take long. No sooner had she entered the front room than Carol described the man whose image was daubed on the wall as being somebody she was picking up on inside the house. She said that his mustache was different in real life—less long and curly than it had been drawn—but that the picture was nonetheless very accurate and lifelike.

The main staircase at the Hostel.

Jason immediately said that when he had first come inside out of the rain, he had experienced something that had never happened to him before in his entire life: the sensation of somebody choking him, trying to squeeze his windpipe shut. I inspected his neck carefully but could detect no signs of redness around his throat.

"Whatever is in here is not nice," he said calmly. He agreed with Carol's assessment that the face smeared on the living room wall was indeed an image of one of the entities that haunted the Hostel.

I accompanied Jason and Carol on a tour of the house, recording Jason's observations as we went. After a brief stop in the mirror room, during which neither of them felt anything, we climbed the rickety wooden steps up to the attic.

The Hanged Man

"Oh—I did not expect that," Jason said as he emerged into the attic behind me.

Before I could ask him what he meant, Carol exclaimed that somebody—a male—had died in this room by hanging. She told us that her throat was beginning to hurt too, which harkened back to what Jason had experienced on first entering the house.

"I've never felt anything this strong before," added Jason, shaking his head. Carol went on to describe an unkempt-looking man whose personal life had spiraled out of control, undergoing a breakup in his relationship and a possible involvement with drugs. The man was showing her a leather belt, she explained, which may have been his method of hanging himself.

Andy confirmed that he had heard stories of a man hanging himself up there in the attic; there were also stories circulating about a ten-year-old boy supposedly being hanged in there too, although there was no evidence for either death that I could find. Jason and Carol were both adamant that this was a man, not a boy, and that he had hung from the rafters for quite a few days before his body was found.

"I can't take it up here anymore. I just can't do it." Carol had to get out of the attic and head downstairs, overcome by the oppressive atmosphere. Jason, Lesley, and I remained for a while. Jason felt that the hanged man had been feeling deeply guilty about something he had done, something which he was trying to either hide from or keep hidden. He believed that the overwhelming guilt finally drove the man to take his own life.

Lesley asked whether the hanged man was the one whose face was on the living room wall. Jason said that it wasn't, as this spirit wasn't malevolent and didn't mean any harm; he was melancholy and guilt-ridden, but not spiteful.

Making our way carefully down the rickety stairs, we continued on with the walk-through. Jason sensed that we were being followed by one of the female entities that haunted the Hostel. Andy confirmed that he often felt the same way when he was alone in the house, getting the distinct sense of somebody dogging his footsteps and watching his every move. None of my instruments were able to detect anything, but I was determined to keep an open mind nonetheless. The psychic went on to describe a young woman with long, curly brown hair dressed in a white ankle-length night dress. She had lost something, Jason told us, and he believed that the "something" was a child.

I asked for clarification—was the child taken in the sense of having died, or had he or she literally been taken away, never to be seen again? Jason was leaning toward the former explanation.

"She was a prisoner here," he explained, "and I think that the male entity whose face is on the wall of the front room is the one who kept her trapped. He's cruel and a bit of a trickster, this one. He doesn't like us being here in his domain, and he'll do anything to get us out."

An Evil Man

Andy mentioned that during past Ouija sessions, the board had told male participants to "f— off." Now Jason's comments started me thinking about our own experiences with the board.

A bit of a trickster…Could this be the reason behind our own garbled Ouija episodes? Jason believed that this was indeed the case; the negative male entity was deliberately messing with us, trying to muddy the waters and playing mind games. That was likely why the Ouija board that I had brought from America with me flatly refused to perform—my wife had asked her grandmother, its original owner, to keep malign influences away from the board.

"This man was very antisocial, a loner," the psychic went on. "I would go so far as to say that he was a genuinely evil man in life, and still is. He did things to entertain himself—mostly to young women—of a very perverse nature. He liked to torture things…It started with animals, but then he graduated to torturing people. All for his own entertainment."

When I asked Jason how old the man had been at the time of his death, he estimated his age at having been either his late sixties or early seventies. Crucially, neither Lesley nor I had told him about the communicator speaking to us via the Ouija board that had claimed to be seventy-three years of age. The image of the man on the wall looked much younger than that, so if Jason had been making this all up based upon the daubing, I would have expected him to have chosen an age several decades younger.

The male entity appeared to be getting angry, as Jason told us that he was telling us all to "f— off." I returned the insult in kind, which, the psychic told me, was just making the nasty man laugh.

While Jason and I had been walking around the ground floor, Carol, Lesley, and some of the others had been spending a little time in the upstairs bedrooms, where Carol said she had sensed what she believed was the spirit of a young girl in the master bedroom, close to the chimney.

From somewhere upstairs, we heard what sounded like a door slam shut. Instinctively, we all looked up, knowing that none of us were up there—every investigator had gathered around the table. I led the team up there, checking each and every one of the doors. All of them were standing open, just as we had left them. Could it perhaps have been a floorboard popping back into place or the structure settling?

"I feel like this has turned into a game of cat and mouse," Andy said. I asked rather pointedly which of us was the cat and which was the mouse.

Jason was now sensing the spirit of a young boy lurking downstairs, occasionally peeking out from his hiding place to look at us. More spirits were emerging, he said, spanning multiple decades of time. He explained that in his opinion, the strong negative energies that were present in the building were serving to attract other spirits like moths to a flame. Carol chimed in that she could psychically "see" children huddling together in twos and threes, living in constant fear of the angry male master of the house. When pushed to give a number of entities currently haunting the house, she said that there were at least twelve.

The Children

Our last night at De Grey Street was fast coming to an end, and so I elected to finish off with a mass EVP session involving all of us in one large group. Making sure that our personal electronic devices were set to airplane mode, we all took up seats around the table and the outer perimeter of the dining room. I set up Stephen the bear in the open doorway of the closet under the stairs, where the spirits of children would supposedly hide.

By unspoken agreement, Carol took the lead. Pointedly ignoring the presence of the angry adult entity, she called out to any child spirits that might be present to come forward and play with us.

"That tickles!" Stephen said, indicating that something was triggering his movement sensors. None of us were moving.

"Come forward," Carol encouraged. "Play with the teddy bear. We're not here to scare you, I promise ..."

"I like hugs!" the bear replied enthusiastically. Movement again. We all remained totally still.

Five minutes passed in silence. We all heard a faint buzz, like somebody humming a tune. In seconds, it was gone. We had to assume that it was somebody walking past outside, heading to the store or to the pub.

Carol and Eileen took turns trying to entice the children out, asking them to make one of our plastic boxes light up. The EMF meters stayed dark.

A heavy thud sounded from somewhere upstairs, much like the one we had mistaken for a door slamming earlier in the night. Needless to say, a search of the upstairs revealed that not a thing was out of place.

No sooner had we all returned to our seats than we heard the sound again, once more coming from up above our heads. The feeling of being played with grew stronger than ever. The air around the table suddenly turned ice-cold. I had a hard time believing it, because it was such a Hollywood thing to happen—a classic staple of the ghost movies. But all of us, with the notable exception of Carol, were feeling it. There were no drafts; looking around the room, I could see that none of the paper we had set out was rustling. Reaching for the closest thermometer, I was able to confirm that the air temperature was indeed dropping, which was the very opposite of what should be happening with so many of us gathered together in one enclosed space, particularly with the heaters operating at full blast.

"Did you make it cold in here?" Stephen the bear asked, offering another means of validation.

"I can hear a baby crying!" Angie suddenly exclaimed. "Upstairs ... it was definitely a cry or a whimper." The sound was so faint that it would not show up on any of our recordings, but this was weeks before I would check the audio files and discover that we had recorded something very similar indeed on the night that Nat had come to investigate with us.

It was getting very late. The activity had reached its high-water mark, and after the baby's cry, it now began to subside. The dining room started to warm up. Stephen stopped speaking, even after a change of batteries. Most importantly of all, our two visiting psychics assured us that the spirits which had been so curious about our presence earlier on in the evening were now beginning to disperse.

We packed up our equipment, returned the keys to Andy, and stepped out into the street for the last time. It was our fifth night at 39 De Grey Street, and I can honestly say that it was an experience I shall never forget. Some members of the paranormal community have scoffed at the idea that the building is haunted, claiming that the entire thing has been cooked up in an attempt to garner publicity and make money. My own experiences there have convinced me that something strange is taking place at 39 De Grey Street, and while it is hardly the house of horrors that the media has made it out to be, I personally have no doubt that it has its ghosts.

After saying our goodbyes, Lesley and I stood outside the place and waited for Andy to lock up. I found myself looking up at the attic window and remembering what Jason had said about the lonely young man who he believed had taken his life up there. Was his restless spirit looking down at me right now, either glad that we were leaving him in peace or even more unhappy now that the only company he had had for so long was now leaving him for good?

Did he even exist at all?

All that I could see was dark glass, and that held no answers.

Nat Goes Back

Over the next few months, Nat would return to the Hostel on several different occasions. She brought a number of guests from her paranormal tour company and documented more bizarre occurrences in the ramshackle old house.

The guests had a host of personal experiences, such as the feeling of being touched and still more of the inexplicable cold spots that I had also encountered, yet the most compelling evidence was captured by an investigator who was operating a Kinect camera system.

If you're not familiar with it, the Kinect is an extremely interesting and useful piece of equipment. It was developed by technology giant Microsoft in order to add an extra dimension of controllability to video games on the Xbox console platform and home computers. Basically, the Kinect is an infrared emitter that is paired with a depth camera and several microphones; the camera is adept at reading the data from the infrared beam, and from that data it can interpret the location of an object (or a person) in the room with a great deal of accuracy. When you stand or sit in front of it, the Kinect is designed to detect that you are there, listen to your voice, and track your movements in time and space.

As with so many pieces of cutting-edge consumer technology, it didn't long for the paranormal research community to latch onto it themselves and use the Kinect in the search to prove the existence of ghosts. If you do even a small amount of online searching, you'll come across numerous accounts of video gamers who have sat down in front of their machines only to find an invisible "companion" sitting next to them, if the Kinect is to be believed. Some technical experts write off these sensory "ghosts" as being false findings, claiming that the Kinect camera is essentially being fooled by shadows and natural patterns of light in the room; others, however, believe that the ghosts on the screen are just that: the spirits of the dead, somehow making their presence known by way of the electronic device.

Rather wisely in my opinion, Microsoft has refused to issue a statement endorsing one point of view over the other. It seems that the true nature of the invisible second player that an increasing number of gamers are reporting will remain a mystery for the foreseeable future.

After hearing some of the Hostel's ghost stories, Nat's guest elected to set up his Kinect in the master bedroom, facing the chimney from which Andy had seen the apparition of the little girl emerge. The device turned out to be useful in an unexpected way: when the baby's crib appeared to start rocking by itself, a replay of the Kinect footage was able to debunk it, proving that a guest had accidentally nudged the crib with their foot in passing.

For the first hour, little of note happened—a few temperature fluctuations, but nothing definitive. The first group of visiting guests left and another rotated in. Toward the end of this second session, the Kinect began to display a human-shaped stick figure standing in the very center of the chimney … a figure that appeared to be floating four feet above the ground.

One intrepid guest stepped forward and extended a hand, requesting that the entity reach out and touch it. The stick figure obliged, reaching down with one arm until the end of it appeared to contact that of the guest.

After a break, the group moved next door to the adjacent children's bedroom. The Kinect went along with it; its owner wanted to see if the spirit they had detected would follow them to this new location. They began an EVP session, which, on immediate playback of the audio files, yielded some definitely anomalous but unclear voices.

Then their new friend returned. Half of this new figure was superimposed against the ceiling, while its bottom half hung down against the wall, its legs stopping some five feet above the floor. This time, the floating figure did not deign to touch the hand of a guest when it was politely asked to do so.

I asked Nat for her overall impressions of the Hostel and its haunted hallways. She wrote back, "I'm now several investigations in at 39 De Grey Street, and whilst I've yet to witness the poltergeist activity which it's built up its reputation for, this location has at least consistently produced activity that we haven't always been able to totally explain. The appearance of the stick figure, mapped out by the Kinect camera, in the exact same place as the owner had seen a ghostly sighting of a little girl certainly is intriguing and has gone a long way in convincing me that the Hostel is indeed haunted."

When it comes to the mythology of 39 De Grey Street, the line between fact and folklore has gotten blurred. Most of the claims about the property's history have to be taken with a big grain of salt and a solid dose of healthy skepticism.

Was it really a hostel or orphanage, as some have claimed? Was it truly used as an overflow morgue during the Second World War? Mike Covell's research makes both propositions seem highly unlikely. Such tales tend to grow in the telling, after all, and much of 39 De Grey Street's fearsome reputation has been built upon anecdote and hearsay. Yet it is impossible to deny that paranormal activity does seem to occur there, and I would challenge those who say otherwise to spend a few nights beneath its leaking roof and crumbling walls to experience the place for themselves.

Hopefully the angry male entity won't take too much of a shine to you ...

CHAPTER 3

FIREHOUSE PHANTOMS

A friend and fellow author was in the process of writing a book about the ghosts of the Denver Firefighters Museum and wanted to know if I would be willing to take my team in there for the night to try to gather some data for her. She had extended the same offer to a number of other local paranormal teams, wanting to cast as wide a net as possible and fully aware that each would bring their own mix of skills, experience, and investigative philosophy to the table.

She didn't need to ask me twice: I jumped at the chance. Despite the fact that BCPRS had investigated the museum back in 2014, it was such an incredible location to simply spend time in that I would have been mad at myself for saying no. As a firefighter, this was a form of hallowed ground to me, full of historic artifacts dating back over more than a hundred and fifty years of Denver firefighting history.

Although it now serves as the departmental museum, the building was the original Denver Fire Station No. 1 when it was constructed in 1909, which operated as a working firehouse until it was decommissioned in 1975.

We were scheduled to start at six o'clock on Saturday evening, and run through until two o'clock the following morning. I was loaded for bear as far as personnel were concerned: senior investigators Jason Fellon, Otis Piper, Seth Woodmansee, and Catlyn Keenan accompanied me and brought along probationary investigators Shane and Jane for their first BCPRS event.

That wasn't all. Two investigators from neighboring teams had also asked to join us for the night, and I was frankly glad to have their help. This wasn't the first rodeo for either Clark or Marvin, and I was also willing to bet that they might teach this old dog one or two new tricks too. That's the beauty of having a team that plays nicely with others: not only do you get to supplement your manpower when more boots on the ground are needed, but it's also an education in how those other teams do things, helping you raise your own game in the process.

Last, there was Mark, or as I should more properly refer to him, Captain Mark Maxwell. We serve on the same volunteer fire department, and I therefore consider him to be a brother, but he also holds the rank of captain at a different fire department. He found the subject of the paranormal intriguing but had never made any serious efforts to get involved. Whenever we served together, Mark made a point of asking me "How's the ghost hunting thing going?" and loved to hear about my latest case, so when the Denver Firefighters Museum popped up on my radar overnight, Mark seemed a natural fit. When I offered to bring him along as an impartial observer, he accepted without hesitation.

There was still a little daylight left when our group assembled on the concrete apron outside the museum, looking up at Old Glory as it flapped in the freshening breeze above our heads. We'd already done a quick walk-around; the building was bordered by an empty, fenced-off lot on one side and a series of apartments on the other. The alleyway out back was narrow and cramped, and we had been warned that it was often the scene of some of Denver's more "interesting" nocturnal activity, something that we would do well to keep away from.

The Funeral Engine

Danielle, a longtime volunteer at the museum, met us with a smile at six o'clock sharp. After unlocking the heavy front door, she let us into the lobby and then closed the door behind us, locking it securely—and shutting us inside the building. She explained that on more than one occasion late-night drinkers had seen lights on inside the museum and crashed through the front door, either just plain curious or wanting to use the restroom.

The museum is located close to Colfax Avenue, one of Denver's most heavily trafficked thoroughfares. It was still early, and we were already hearing the wail of sirens as police cruisers, fire trucks, and ambulances rocketed by, heading toward who-knew-what emergency. The siren's song would be a constant backdrop throughout the course of our investigation, and we soon reached a point at which we were all just tuning it out.

Danielle gave us a guided tour of all three levels. Despite the fact that we had both been visitors there before, Mark and

I were like two kids in a candy store, wandering around with broad grins plastered on our faces.

The ground floor was mostly taken up with the apparatus bay, where fire engines and old horse-drawn pumper apparatus and hook-and-ladder carts sat alongside one another, all of them lovingly restored and refurbished to a highly polished sheen. Engine 4, a 1950s-era antique that still ran like a charm, had been used that same day, representing the Denver Fire Department in the city's St. Patrick's Day parade.

"What are these used for?" I asked, lightly touching the black fabric curtain that was rolled up and hung from the side of the hose bed. Danielle suddenly turned very serious.

"Engine 4 is used for department funerals," she explained, "and is used to take either fallen firefighters or retired ones to their final resting place."

We all went quiet, not really sure of what to say. I took a peek at the hose bed and saw that in the place where a normal in-service fire engine would have hundreds of feet of supply hose and attack line, there was instead a metal frame that could have only one purpose: to hold a funeral casket securely in place for one somber, final ride on the engine for a faithful servant of the fire department.

"There are some interesting photos connected with this engine," Danielle said, ushering us over to a computer monitor and firing up a sequence of three images. They had obviously all been taken with the same camera, by a photographer who hadn't moved at all. Each picture showed the side tailboard of Engine 4. "They were taken by a visiting paranormal group."

The first was unremarkable, showing nothing but the tail-board and a chrome handrail. On the second, something neb-ulous and white could just be glimpsed in between the handrail and the frame of the fire engine itself. And the third...

Well, the third time's the charm, as the old saying goes. As-suming that the photograph was not a fake, something generated by Photoshop or some similar type of image manipulation soft-ware, then the paranormal group that took the picture may well have captured a full-bodied apparition on camera.

Whatever it was, the focus of the picture seemed to be moving very quickly. It was an indistinct form, tall, white, and semitrans-parent. The second photo seemed to show the object entering the frame from the left-hand side, showing just a glimpse of the fig-ure's leading edge. The third photo had caught the figure in full charge, barreling from left to right at high speed.

We clustered around the monitor and squinted, our faces scrunching up in masks of concentration as we tried to figure out just what exactly we were looking at. Mark thought that he could see the form of a firefighter perhaps, whereas others thought that it looked more like a female figure in a dress. Danielle told us that the museum staff leaned more toward it being a female apparition and always referred to it as a female. For my part, I also thought it looked more like a woman in a dress than a firefighter. In fact, while it's entirely possible that my eyes were seeing patterns in something that wasn't actually there, I really thought that I could make out a thin forearm and a hand gathering a long skirt up at her waist, as though she were making sure not to trip over the hem as she moved quickly across the floor of the apparatus bay.

But that begged the question, why would the ghost of a woman from a bygone age be found haunting such a male-centric environment as a firehouse-turned-museum? Although women are well represented in the modern-day fire service, such was not the case during the years when this was an active DFD firehouse.

One possibility comes in the form of a potential link between her and Engine 4. Could she perhaps be the widow of a fire-fighter whose casket was transported on that very same hose bed, for example? While possible, that explanation alone seems like something of a stretch to me ... at least, until we consider the fact that there were women and also children around the firehouse on a fairly regular basis. During its formative years in the late nineteenth and early twentieth centuries, the firemen worked extremely long shifts that kept them away from home for days at a time. Cognizant of the fact that this would be difficult on their marriages and the raising of their children, the department made sure that a family room was available in most firehouses; this was a sort of hybrid between a kitchenette and a living room, where each fireman's family could come and visit him while he was on duty, with a door that could be closed to allow a little privacy even in the middle of the hustle and bustle of firehouse life.

Could the figure in the photo actually be that of a fireman's wife who spent time at the station with her husband, keeping him company for as long as possible before he was forced to race to the pole when the alarm bells sounded, throwing on his turn-out gear and rushing off to answer the call?

We may never know the answer, but I made a mental note to make Engine 4 a focal point of our investigation that night.

Respecting the Sacred

Danielle escorted us upstairs next. Even though I knew what was coming, I still found the experience overwhelming. We were walking into a treasure trove of historic fire service memorabilia imbued with such incredible meaning and poignancy that it almost brought tears to my eyes. I stood mutely before what at first glance looked like a scrap of twisted iron but was actually a section of structural metal from the World Trade Center. Images of the FDNY heroes who had responded to the tragic events of 9/11 were scattered throughout the museum and served as a constant reminder of the ultimate sacrifice that those who wear bunker gear are sometimes called upon to make.

There were also the helmets of two firefighters who had been caught in a severe fire back in the 1980s. Both sets of protective leather headgear were burned almost beyond recognition, warped and twisted by the extreme heat to which they had been exposed, and I was both sickened and relieved to learn that the two firefighters to which they belonged had escaped from the fire alive—but were horrifically burned in the process.

Then there was the mattress upon which the soot-stained outline of a human body could clearly be seen, a stark reminder of the dangers of smoking in bed; the heat-warped and mangled toy fire truck; and perhaps most poignant of all, the roll-call of all those firefighters who had given their lives in service to the people of Denver since the department's inception.

Mark and I exchanged a knowing look. Nothing needed to be said. Nevertheless, I gathered my crew up, because I did feel that something needed to be said to them.

"Guys, we're always a very respectful team," I began, searching for the right words so that I would not offend any of them. "I never worry about your behavior on a location, because despite having a sense of humor, you're still always professional, no matter what. But this place is different." I made sure to make eye contact with each and every one of them in order to emphasize my point. "I'm not a religious man, but this is the closest thing I've got to a sacred place.

"Please remember that every artifact in here, every piece of apparatus, every helmet and piece of bunker gear or tool—all of it is steeped in the history and tradition of the fire service. One of our brothers or sisters has struggled, sweated, and sometimes bled in this gear, and it has deep meaning for us. So please do me a huge favor and treat it with an extra level of respect, okay?"

Just as I had expected, there was no grumbling or even good-natured ribbing. There were simply nods of assent.

Danielle led us over to a large U-shaped table, where she told us that other teams had gotten great results when using spirit boxes. I made a mental note of that. Two small rooms flanked the table on either side of the open hallway.

These were the captains' quarters, and the rooms looked very different from one another.

The first had been restored to its former glory, with a polished wooden wardrobe and an iron-framed bed. A beautifully carved writing desk stood in one corner, home to an old-fashioned typewriter and a series of books and ledgers bound in leather. This was where the captain of the engine would live and sleep, Danielle explained, a little corner of privacy away from his men where he could carry out the administrative tasks so familiar to every fire officer since time immemorial.

The second room, on the other hand, wasn't getting much love at all. This was the quarters of the hook and ladder company captain, whose firemen did a different—but every bit as hazardous—job from those who rode the engine. These were the men who went to the roof in order to ventilate the super-heated smoke and gases and threw ladders quickly up against windows in an effort to "make a grab"—to save the life of a civilian who was trapped by the onrushing smoke and flame. Today, these men and women are affectionately known as "truckies," and a healthy rivalry exists between them and the engine crews, just as it always has.

The hook and ladder captain's room had definitely seen better days. One window was broken and covered over with cardboard, letting in a draft. Cardboard boxes were stacked high against one wall, and pieces of old and disused equipment were strewn about the room. It looked like more of a junk room than the quarters of a fire officer, and the thought saddened me a little. It seemed vaguely disrespectful, even though I knew that the museum staff didn't intend it that way.

"Let me know if you get anything...unusual in here," Danielle told us with a faint smile, refusing to be drawn further when one of my team asked for a little more detail. "I'll tell you at the end of the night."

Fair enough, I thought as she led us all downstairs to the basement. This was the administrative center of the museum, where the staff had their own computer desks and workspaces. There were also archives of fire service publications going back decades.

Caleb's Closet

The resident spirit down here was a preteen boy named Caleb, we learned, who was believed to have Down syndrome. He was a gentle spirit that was most commonly encountered around the stationary closet, and Danielle insisted several times that we really had to respect him and respect his space. After all, the last time somebody hadn't done that, they had gotten hurt.

"What do you mean, 'hurt'?" I asked, fascinated. Danielle went on to tell us that two members of another paranormal team had shut themselves inside Caleb's closet and, while they had been less than forthcoming about what they had actually been doing inside there, it had obviously gotten them on Caleb's bad side: one of them had been slammed forcefully into the wall, causing them both to flee the closet—and the basement—as fast as their legs would carry them.

I assured her that we were a respectful team and wouldn't be stirring up any trouble with Caleb. Danielle seemed relieved and went on to tell us about the understanding she had cultivated with the museum ghosts over the years. In short, she didn't bother them, and in return they didn't bother her...except for the time when the visitors had made Caleb angry. She had found herself all alone in the basement that night, with the rest of the building empty, and was just about to leave when the lights turned themselves off, plunging her into complete darkness down there.

Knowing that she was all alone and with her heart pounding hard in her chest, she made her way slowly to the staircase that would take her upstairs, apologizing to Caleb every step of the way. "We've been good ever since," she laughed, adding that she had already let Caleb know of our presence in advance, and that if we behaved ourselves, then he would too.

With that, it was time to go to work.

Later on, we'd split up and cover all three levels simultaneously. First things first, though: I wanted to see if all ten of us, massed together around the U-shaped table on the second floor, would be able to get any kind of result. I was reasoning that the combined energy of ten people could be quite the fuel source for anything that wanted to manifest.

While I fired up the SB11 Spirit Box and set it to sweeping its way through the AM and FM radio frequencies, Marvin unpacked a special sleeve that acted a lot like a Faraday cage. Its sole job was to keep out stray radio signals, thus reducing the possibility of outside interference if the spirit box began to speak. I slipped the SB11 into the sleeve and set it carefully down on the tabletop, alongside a K2 meter and a digital voice recorder.

Then we killed the lights.

The harsh, staccato sounds of the spirit box cycling through frequencies were broken only by the sound of my teammates and me asking questions. Jason began, inviting any spirits present to make themselves known to us. I've had some good results with the box over the years, hearing my name and those of my friends come through it sometimes and on one memorable occasion even being called an asshole! But tonight, it simply wasn't to be. For fifteen solid minutes we plied it with questions and were greeted with nothing but the sound of static.

We got one exception: about ten minutes in, we heard what sounded like a male voice saying the name "Dave." Everybody's ears perked up at that, but when we tried to find out more, the box remained stubbornly unhelpful.

"It might help if we take it out of the sleeve," Marvin said doubtfully, knowing full well that if he did so, it was going to open the device up to the entire gamut of commercial and private radio frequencies. Still, what we were doing right now wasn't working, so what did we have to lose?

Apparently, everything. Now we were hearing random snippets of radio stations, each one gone in the space of a heartbeat, but nothing intelligible. The box was refusing to play ball tonight, it seemed. Finally admitting defeat after thirty minutes had gone by, I grudgingly accepted that it was probably time to get the ball rolling on the investigation proper.

I divided my team up into three groups. That would give me the latitude to cover all three floors simultaneously, and we'd be backed up by the museum security camera system if anything anomalous put in an appearance ... like the lady in the apparatus bay.

Catlyn and Jane, our two female investigators, opted to band together for the evening. They formed my first team. My second comprised Jason, Seth, and Marvin, with our guest Clark tagging along, and the third and final team was made up of Otis, his probie Shane, and Captain Maxwell.

Off We Go

The clock was creeping up on nine when the teams finally trooped off to their first locations. The women went downstairs to the basement, hoping to connect with the spirit of young Caleb; Otis's team stayed on the ground floor, electing to focus their attentions on Engine 4; and Jason led his crew upstairs, wanting to devote some time to the engine captain's quarters.

Now we ran into the first major problem of the investigation: communications. Each team had been issued a walkie-talkie before they headed out. We'd performed a radio check, confirming that we were all operating on the same channel, and had no problems before splitting up. I could hear the tread of boots on the ceiling above me and knew that Jason's team was in place. I could see Otis and his guys across the bay next to Engine 4 and figured that Catlyn and Jane had to be in place downstairs by now.

Keying up the radio, I couldn't hear anything except for squelch and static, just like the spirit box. This was ridiculous: I could see Otis, not thirty feet away. Yet when I tried to talk to him over the walkie-talkie, it sounded as though he was at the bottom of a deep, dark well, and I had to strain my ears to make out even a single word.

That was the best radio communication we had all night. For the guys upstairs and downstairs, nothing could be heard but the occasional click of a handset being keyed. Grumbling, I went to each of the three teams in turn and gave them a manual start time, and a finish time thirty minutes later. That was the only way we'd be able to coordinate our activities, because the radios—and we had eight of them in order to rule out mechanical or electrical issues—flat-out failed to do their job.

The first rotation was mostly uneventful. Despite their best efforts, nothing my teammates did seemed to entice the spirits out of hiding. It wasn't that they hadn't tried. Down in the basement, Catlyn and Jane had tried their best to make a connection with young Caleb, even going so far as to break out some toys for him to play with.

Otis, Shane, and Mark were unable to figure out the reason for Engine 4 registering so high on their EMF meters, finally giving up when they ruled out all nearby artificial energy sources as the cause. Taking some initiative, Mark read aloud the names of the fallen firefighters from a snapshot he'd taken of the list upstairs. From my place in the operations center, I could hear him respectfully intoning the names of the fallen in a calm, reverential manner and had to wipe a tear or two away with my sleeve.

Upstairs, Jason's team had conducted an EVP session in the engine officer's quarters and had gotten no phenomena of any kind. The evidence review of the audio data later on would turn up a big fat zero too.

Everybody was getting thirsty because we were obeying the museum's "no food or drinks around the artifacts" rule to the letter, and so it was only after a water break that the three groups traded places. The women came up to the ground floor, Otis's team went up to the officer's quarters, and Jason and his crew went down to the basement.

Things were little better the second time around. The only thing that came even close to unusual happened with Otis's team up in the captain's quarters. Mark had talked respectfully but candidly about some of the more challenging aspects of being a fire officer. This ranged from how to motivate the lazier fire recruit all the way up to making life-or-death decisions, the consequences of which sometimes turned out badly. They were rewarded with some K2 activity, sometimes flashing up into the three- and four-light range when Mark asked for answers.

This sounded encouraging at first, but the problem with it was that the entire upper floor of the Denver Firefighters Museum might best be described as "an EMF nightmare." On both of my visits, and those of the other teams that I'd talked to, pretty much everybody had been tearing their hair out when trying to use EMF meters up there. Some areas were basically inert, but others had ridiculously high levels of electromagnetic energy, burying the needle of a Trifield meter.

To make matters even worse, the energy fields were dynamic: they fluctuated, expanding and contracting with no apparent rhyme or reason as time went on. That meant that, despite the fact that Mark's K2 results were interesting, we really had to write them off as a part of the generally erratic EMF background activity that plagued the upper floor. It did, however, raise a few eyebrows when Jason pointed out that his team hadn't gotten a single K2 spike in that same room.

We're Being Watched

We were to have better luck on our third rotation. Catlyn and Jane came up to the second floor and, heeding Danielle's advice, elected to spend their time in the officer's quarters. Both reported feeling distinctly uneasy in there, but they were unable to gather any objective evidence to support what was a totally subjective sensation.

"We felt like we were being watched," Jane explained sheepishly afterward. "It was as if there was a pair of eyes watching me wherever I went in there." The cold draft may have offered a partial explanation, but when Danielle came to join us afterward, she added some intriguing perspective.

Over the past few years, many people claiming to have psychic or sensitive capabilities had remarked upon the negative, almost oppressive energies in that same room: some had flatly refused to even step foot in there, citing a dark and heavy atmosphere when approaching the threshold. Jane and Catlyn were now the latest pair of names to be added to that list.

On the ground floor, Jason's team had struck out for a third time in the apparatus bay, but Otis's team had fared better down in the basement. While trying to connect with Caleb, probationary member Shane had suddenly experienced a weakening in his legs. He sat down quickly before he fell down, and then was overcome with a wave of what he described afterward as "absolutely blissful joy and love." His mind went straight to his own children, and he felt a huge grin spreading across his face.

"Does Shane remind you of somebody?" Otis had asked into thin air. He wasn't expecting a reply, but he got one: a high-pitched squeak that sounded like a child saying "hmmm." All three men heard the noise and agreed that it sounded as if it had an organic origin rather than an artificial one; in other words, this wasn't the creaking of a pipe or the sound of the structure settling. By their best estimation, it had originated from down inside the basement with them, in an isolated corner. When the audio file was reviewed later, the sound had been recorded, but was extremely faint and difficult to make out.

Then there came a knock from the same part of the basement.

"Can you do that again?" Otis asked optimistically. The answer was apparently yes, because a second knock followed hard on the heels of the first. Despite searching the basement from top to bottom, no source for the noises was anywhere to be found.

At the debrief afterward, all three investigators remained convinced that the noises were of paranormal origin...or at the very least, that they could not be explained away by conventional means.

The night was fast drawing to a close. Our investigation was going to be cut short because the clocks were due to be set forward at 2 a.m. It was time for them to "spring ahead" an extra hour, and Danielle wanted to get home. For the last phase of the night, we split into two teams. Half of the investigators went upstairs to divide themselves between the two captains' quarters, and the other half—including myself—elected to head down to the basement in an attempt to get Caleb to speak to us.

Before traveling to the fire museum that night, I had put fresh batteries in all of my equipment and fully charged everything with an internal battery. Now, pulling out my full-spectrum GoPro camera from its case, I saw that it had been completely drained without ever being switched on. This is far from unusual on paranormal investigations, and I have seen it happen countless times during my twenty years in the field. Nonetheless, it made me groan with frustration, and I traded the now-useless lump of plastic for a FLIR (forward-looking infrared) thermal camera, something that could literally see in the dark.

Killing the basement lights, I settled in with Catlyn, Otis, and Shane for a vigil directly outside Caleb's stationary cupboard. Scanning around with the FLIR, I could see my fellow investigators glowing in shades of fiery red, yellow, and orange, with the colder spots around them contrasting in a series of blues, blacks, and purples.

Of Caleb, however, there was no sign.

Suddenly, I heard a low moan. Excitedly, I swung the camera around in the direction that it had seemed to come from—and found the source. Shane had his head in his hands and was slumped back against the wall, half-sitting on his haunches in an attempt to support his weight.

"Are you okay, buddy?" Otis asked.

"Feel nauseous," Shane slurred. "Might throw up."

Catlyn was by his side in a second. "He's burning up," she said worriedly, placing a hand across his forehead. "He's almost fever hot."

I frowned. The basement was warm, certainly, but not hot. Shane had been overcome all of a sudden. Otis agreed that Shane's skin seemed to be burning up when he touched it.

I made a command decision. "Let's move him over there," I said, then realized how stupid that was because the basement was in absolute darkness. Pointing with the FLIR unit toward the basement staircase, Catlyn and Otis helped Shane move to a different spot.

"Starting to feel better," Shane said almost immediately, though he did take the opportunity to remove his hoodie. Catlyn had replaced him in the spot outside Caleb's closet.

"Was that you, Caleb?" she asked. "Can you make me feel the same way?"

Despite her best efforts, she wasn't able to exhort Caleb to come out and play with her, nor would he speak or knock on any surfaces. Shane made a full and immediate recovery and remained nonplussed about the cause of his sudden episode. Although he had consumed an energy drink that night, he had also been hydrating with water. The only location in which he had been physically affected remained the basement; he had been absolutely fine on the ground and second floors.

At that point, we called a halt to the proceedings and reunited with the second group. They had experienced nothing unusual upstairs, and Mark had been unable to replicate the K2 results in the engine captain's quarters—the room was now totally inert, as though something had been in there but had left.

Packing up our gear and saying goodbye to Danielle, we left the museum with more questions than answers, but also some very fond memories. As a firefighter of fifteen years' service, I felt enormously privileged to have been allowed to spend the night in one of Denver's oldest and most historic firehouses.

A firehouse is a family. Firefighters work, sleep, train, play, laugh, and sometimes cry together. The job has its high and low points, and I can state from personal experience that the highs tend to be very high indeed (the elation that comes at having saved a life) and the lows are very low, thanks to some of the truly horrific situations that firefighters are exposed to. We see life, death, and everything in between. Imagine the sheer volume of intense emotion that is experience by the inhabitants of a place such as the original Denver Fire Station No. 1.

No wonder it has its ghosts. The building—along with more than a few of the brave men who lived and worked within it, I suspect—is unquestionably haunted.

After all, ghosts come in many different forms...

CHAPTER 4

GOING UNDERGROUND

Even paranormal investigators like to enjoy a little working holiday every now and then.

It had been a while since I had gotten back to the United Kingdom, and I was beginning to get a little bit homesick. I began planning a trip back across the pond, with a view to visiting some haunted locations while I was over there. Why not kill two birds with one stone?

As I began to line up some interesting places to investigate, my good friends and fellow paranormal investigators Jason and Linda Fellon mentioned that they had always wanted to visit the UK. When I asked if they would like to accompany me, they jumped at the chance, which is how the three of us found ourselves getting off a plane at Heathrow Airport on a swelteringly hot July day.

Our first night was to be spent in London itself. In order to start coping with the inevitable jet lag, we had planned to take it easy and have an early night before driving to the first location on our itinerary the following morning.

That wasn't how things actually turned out.

Friendly Spirits

Nothing beats a pint of warm British beer in a friendly pub. Many of Britain's pubs have their own resident ghost (or at the very least, ghost story—the spook itself may have long since departed!).

My first pit stop in London is usually the Westminster Arms, located just around the corner from Westminster Abbey and the Houses of Parliament. Although I've never encountered him personally, the pub is supposedly haunted by the ghost of a young boy. Charred and blistered as if he were killed in a fire, this sad specter is seen wandering forlornly in the vicinity of this drinking haunt for politicians and reporters, possibly looking for his parents. The tales do not tell us how he died, but there are vague legends about a building fire back in the seventeenth century in which he is said to have burned to death.

After checking into our hotel, we always head for a swift pint or two at the Arms. I was looking forward to introducing Jason and Linda to the place, but unfortunately it happened to be closed for the day.

Fortunately, one of my favorite pubs in the entire world was open: the charming and unquestionably haunted Grenadier.

The Guardsman is the original name of this beautiful old watering hole, once the officers' mess for the First Regiment of Foot Guards, which dates back to 1720; yet the current name of the Grenadier fits just as well. After the military establishment was converted into a public house, the pub's name was subsequently changed in the aftermath of the decisive Battle of Waterloo, in which the Duke of Wellington dealt Napoleon Bonaparte his final defeat.

The pub's painted sign depicts the image of a mustachioed, bearskin-wearing guardsman glowering sternly down at the patrons as they enter and leave. If you head out into Old Barrack Yard, which is the pub's side entrance, you can still see (and stand on!) a block of stone that is reputed to be the Duke of Wellington's mounting step, which he used as an aid to climb up onto his horse.

Finding the Grenadier can be a bit of a challenge, unless you happen to know exactly where to look. The pub is one of the capital's best-kept open secrets. The armies of tourists that invade London on a regular basis usually miss the place because it's hidden away on a backstreet in a rather exclusive area named Wilton Mews (the singer Madonna is known to drop in for a drink every once in a while). It's easiest to reach on foot, taking a couple of backstreets and side alleys until you reach Old Barrack Yard, where the Foot Guards are said to have conducted their drill sessions, or the front entrance by Wilton Row.

Stepping inside is like going back in time. The place looks, smells, and more importantly feels like a pub ought to. Wooden paneling adorns the walls and brassware and various regimental memorabilia of the Grenadier Guards are distributed throughout the place. It was comfortably quiet when we stepped inside, which gave Jason and Linda the chance to wander around the pub interior and check out the many framed newspaper clippings that hang all around the place. The articles go back for several decades, and most of them focus on the paranormal activity for which the Grenadier has become world famous.

Landlords, landladies, and bar staff have reported ghostly goings-on at the Grenadier for years. The tale behind this originates with the pub allegedly being the officers' mess for a Guards regiment in the years leading up to the Battle of Waterloo. In such days the "gentlemen's code" to which the army officers adhered allowed such men to get away with many transgressions that would be frowned upon by the rest of society. But there was one great unpardonable crime for which an officer could never be forgiven—an act of dishonor.

Cheating at cards was regarded as such an act. The story goes that sometime in September during the nineteenth century, one very junior officer was caught cheating in a card game. Outraged, his peer officers beat the poor fellow almost to death, battering him until he was bloody and employing whips once his uniform had been torn off. Staggering down to the cellar, the luckless officer breathed his last and expired on the cold stone floor.

This haunting contains some of the elements usually found within an anniversary case. Successive tenants of the Grenadier tell of paranormal activity occurring throughout the year but building gradually to an apparent peak around the month of September, then dying down over Christmas, and building again the following year. Certainly, both staff and customers have witnessed the blurry apparition of a Georgian-era soldier (usually upon the staircase) and also an indefinable black shape drifting throughout the pub.

Lights and electrical devices go haywire. Knocking sounds echo throughout the pub, with no apparent cause. Plumbing issues can also be a problem, such as taps switching themselves on and off. Cold spots and icy drafts are commonplace. Domestic animals go a little crazy, particularly in the area of the cellar. Objects move by apparently unseen hands. Strange mists and foggy clouds have been reported by a number of witnesses, and odd effects can occur in photographs taken in and around the Grenadier.

The landlord was kind enough to allow us down into the cellar, one of the more paranormally active parts of the pub. We spent a few minutes talking about one of the many tales associated with the Grenadier, a secret tunnel that is supposed to link the Grenadier with the Duke of Wellington's home at Apsley House, which has the unique address of Number One, London.

We couldn't find the entrance to a tunnel, and so the three of us went back upstairs to enjoy another round of drinks while we waited for lunch to arrive. Relaxing back in his chair and sipping at his drink, Jason happened to look up. "What's going on with the ceiling?" he asked.

One lovely tradition has arisen with respect to the haunting backstory at the Grenadier. Tourists from around the world (many of them paranormal enthusiasts) seek out the pub when they come to London, and many of them leave something behind when they leave.

Glued to the ceiling is a massive collage of bank notes that originate from a host of different countries. Most of the notes have the name of their former owner written on them. The tradition is that visitors from foreign shores leave a donation to help release the Grenadier's resident lost soul, in an attempt to help him pay off his gambling debt. Perhaps then the ghostly grenadier officer can finally find his eternal rest. If you happen to drop by and visit this most haunted of historic pubs, be sure to take a look for my five-dollar bill nestled somewhere among the mass of crumpled notes.

We had just begun to dig in to our food when I received a text. It was from my friend Dave, who was a train driver on the London Underground. He was making us an offer we just couldn't refuse.

The Plague Pits

"How would you guys like to investigate a haunted London Underground station's power house?" I asked Jason and Linda.

"Oh, heck yes!" they chorused.

"Then let's eat up. We've got a train to catch."

Stopping only to grab our cases of equipment, we set out for an overnight investigation beneath the streets of London.

The closest Underground station to the Grenadier is Hyde Park Corner, which has its own reputation for being haunted by the sound of girls sobbing, though none are ever found when the braver members of staff go to investigate. The station is renowned for having a number of ice-cold spots all year round, even in the sweltering heat of summer. Speaking off the record, some of the Underground staff have told investigators and authors that they have felt the distinct sensation of being watched; they get a strong impression that whoever is watching them is decidedly malevolent.

Dave had given us directions to the proper station and promised to meet us there. Also joining us would be his wife Lesley, whom I worked with before when we investigated the Cage, a haunted witches' prison in Essex.

To say that we were excited would be a massive understatement. The London Underground has a tremendous reputation for being haunted, with countless accounts of ghost sightings and other paranormal activity. As our train sped toward its destination, the three of us talked about some of the more notable ones.

It's hardly surprising that the subterranean railroad network is said to be haunted. One only has to look at the ground from which it was excavated to appreciate the reasons why: burial pits abound across the sprawling network, used to inter the bodies of those who died of the plague.

Part of the Piccadilly Line had to be excavated around a massive burial pit, where the skeletal human remains were packed together so tightly that it was impossible to dig through them.

Aldgate Station sits practically on top of a massive plague pit, whose corpses number in the thousands. Excavation in the area has turned up hundreds of coffins, some of which were stuffed with as many as five bodies each; this cramped manner of burial was not uncommon during the days in which the Black Death stalked the streets of Aldgate, when funerals were hasty and perfunctory affairs.

Many of those bodies lie just beyond the wall of the London Underground tunnels to this very day, almost close enough for the hundreds of thousands of commuters to reach out and touch. Do their restless souls still wander along the railway tracks, perhaps, invisible witnesses to the comings and goings of our everyday world? Workers at Aldgate often speak of phantom footsteps approaching them in the semideserted tunnels late at night, their sound usually trailing away as they reach the disbelieving eyewitness.

Liverpool Street Station also sits atop a burial pit, thanks to the fact that it was constructed on the site of a former hospital. The manic screams of a woman are sometimes heard echoing around the station walls and are believed to belong to a patient of that hospital, still suffering from her maladies centuries after her death.

Several apparitions have been reported at Liverpool Street over the years, including at least one that was spotted on the station's closed-circuit TV camera system ... but not by the employee who was sent to investigate.

During the horrific terror attacks in the summer of 2005, a train close to the station was tragically destroyed with great loss of life when a suicide bomber detonated an explosive device on board.

Liverpool Street is not the only station to experience its share of tragedy. Ever since the Second World War, Bethnal Green Station has been haunted by the terrified screams of women and children, perhaps an echo of the disaster that took place on the night of March 3, 1943, when 173 civilians (the majority of them women and children) stampeded into the station in a blind panic. Most were crushed to death in the narrow and cramped confines of the station's entrance. To make matters worse, the presumed air raid that had sparked the panic turned out to be a false alarm; those poor souls had died for no reason.

Barry's Story

Lesley very much wanted to be a part of the investigation, so she and Dave met us when we arrived at our destination, which I will refer to simply as "the power house" as a courtesy to those who still work there and may not want it to be identified.

After a round of hugs, Dave introduced us to Barry Oakley, who was to be our host for the evening. A longtime employee of the London Underground, Barry had an abiding interest in all things paranormal after having had several inexplicable experiences himself over the years. An intelligent and well-spoken man, he has appeared in a television documentary titled *Ghosts on the Underground*, which was narrated by former *Doctor Who* star Paul McGann, in which Barry talked about his ghostly encounters.

Dave didn't have much time for the paranormal, and after leaving us in Barry's capable hands, he headed home for the evening, promising to pick us up the following morning once we had finished our investigation. Barry led us inside to the staff break room and offered us tea and coffee. Before we started work, I wanted to take the opportunity to pick our host's brains regarding the haunting of London's sprawling underground network, which spans over 250 miles of railroad track.

After we mentioned that we had visited the Grenadier before heading to Hyde Park Corner, Barry revealed his own experience at that particular station back in the late 1970s. Working overnight, one of his duties was to remove the breakers from the escalators in order to stop them operating. Having taken care of that particular task, he went back to his office. At 2:30 a.m., he and a fellow employee heard a commotion going on outside in the station.

Heading out to investigate, Barry and his colleague were amazed to find that the escalator was up and running... even though Barry had removed the breakers. Without that component in place, it was theoretically impossible for the escalator to draw any electrical power at all—not to mention the fact that it was necessary to use a specific key in order to start up the escalator, a key that was in Barry's possession.

Admittedly a little spooked by the strange event, Barry did what most Brits will do after receiving a shock: he made himself and his equally shaken colleague a cup of tea. While he was waiting for the kettle to boil, Barry became convinced that there was another presence in the room with them both. He felt the air temperature suddenly drop, feeling a chill wash over his body.

Turning slowly, Barry looked at his coworker. The man was obviously terrified, having turned as white as a sheet and using a table to support himself. Barry could see that the poor soul was shaking.

"Whatever's the matter?" he asked. Shaking his head, his colleague clammed up and refused to speak. It took a good ten minutes and a steaming hot cup of tea for Barry to coax the story out of him.

While Barry's back had been turned, his colleague had watched aghast as the head of a man had drifted through the wall of the supervisor's office. It floated in the air for a moment, looking at both of the London Underground employees in silence, before finally fading away. The poor eyewitness had been paralyzed with fear, unable to move or speak. Barry had felt the presence but had done his best to brush it off and get on with the business of making the tea.

His nerves having gotten the better of him, Barry's petrified colleague quite understandably decided to call it a night, clocking off early and going home. Shortly afterward he decided that a change in career was in order, and he left the Underground for good. Barry said, "Our linemen, the men who walk the track in pairs at night carrying a lantern, sometimes see a figure with a light coming toward them in the tunnels. Those tunnels are meant to be empty, and the figures always disappear in the darkness before the linemen can identify them..."

Shadow Man

We were lapping up Barry's anecdotes about the ghosts of the Underground—I could honestly have sat there all night and just listened—but we were losing daylight, so I asked him to tell us a little about the power house we were now investigating. It was a tall and imposing building set against the railroad track.

"This used to be a substation in the 1800s, but they converted it into administrative offices and crew rooms a few years back," he explained, "so all the walls are lined with lead that is eighteen inches thick."

I found that particularly interesting in terms of any EMF readings we might get that night—lead doesn't do much to block radio waves, so I didn't anticipate it being much of a problem. After all, it wasn't as if we were going to run any X-rays.

Barry went on to tell us that when the building was converted from being a substation into its present form, the interior structure was completely gutted by the construction workers. A photograph was taken inside the dark and empty shell of a building by an employee, and it showed the silhouette of a man standing in the shadows, simply staring back at the photographer. Due to the figure's pose, there was no possibility of it actually having been the photographer himself—at the time of writing the mysterious man's identity remains unknown.

To this day a number of Barry's colleagues dislike working in the old substation late at night, where doors have been known to open and close by themselves. Staff have also heard the drawers of filing cabinets squeaking open and slamming shut when nobody is present in the offices. The building lights also seem to have a penchant for switching themselves on and off on occasion.

He admitted that even he, a man who had worked at some of London Underground's most haunted stations, did not like going down into the basement sometimes. Barry couldn't quite shake the feeling that something was down there with him and was convinced that something bad must have happened down there in the past. His suspicion is that the ghost is a former employee who passed away inside the building back when it was a substation, although that is purely conjecture on his part.

Barry told us of the morning when he had caught a glimpse of a figure walking straight through one of the walls inside the building, though he did hasten to add that it might just have been a trick of the light or his mind. I found his willingness to advance a non-paranormal explanation refreshing and indicative of his reliability as a witness in my opinion. When Barry went after the figure, thinking that it may have been a train driver, he found the building to be empty.

When I asked him why he thought the station might be paranormally active, he responded with a fascinating theory. Tens of thousands of volts of electricity run through the power lines nearby. Wouldn't that make an easy and practically limitless source of energy for an entity to use in order to manifest? We had to admit that it would indeed: it was practically an endless buffet of free power.

Down Below

We all agreed that the basement appeared to be the focus of the haunting here, and so Barry led us down there in single file. It was a wide-open expanse of cement and concrete supported by a series of pillars. The ceiling was extremely low in places. Our host made sure that the door was secure behind the last person, locking us in and, more importantly, locking out any human intruders that might interrupt our investigation.

The air down there was quite cool, which was a little unusual for London at the height of summer.

"Sometimes I just can't wait to get out of here," Barry said with a shudder. He revealed that whenever it was necessary for him to visit the basement in order to test the fire alarm system, he would never go down there alone and would only stay exactly long enough to run the test.

We set about baselining with EMF meters and thermometers. Surprisingly, there were very few electromagnetic hotspots at all, with the obvious exception of some power circuits. The basement was almost inert so far as our K2 meters and Trifields were concerned, which was not what I would have expected at all. That would make it easier for our investigation and also made it less likely that Barry's feelings of disquiet and being watched could be put down to the natural effects of high EMF on the human brain.

Barry directed us to the spot where he usually felt most uncomfortable, and we each pulled up a piece of floor, forming a rough circle. Linda kicked off our EVP session while Jason began calling out for any entities to make their presence known.

A knock came from somewhere off to our right. I asked Barry whether that was a normal mechanical sound for this basement. He shook his head solemnly.

Suddenly, a deep, bass rumble made everybody but Barry look up in surprise. With a smile, he told us that a train was coming into the station. He knew every natural sound of the old substation like the back of his hand.

"I know that you are here," Barry said to thin air, "because I can feel you when I come down here. Will you please let us know that you actually exist?"

Something between a hiss and a snap came from the shadows behind us. Barry assured us that it was not a normal sound, and that he had heard nothing like it down here before. I shone the beam of my flashlight in that direction, but all I could see was the far wall.

Lesley asked for the spirit to give us its name. The Ovilus, a device that senses electromagnetic energy levels in the surrounding environment and maps them to a specific word in its database, had not spoken a word up until then but promptly came out with the name *Rodger.*

"I get the strong feeling that this man died in his early 70s," Barry said, "because I keep getting the number 72 in my head somehow."

We took turns in calling out, trying to get the spirit of the man—assuming that he was actually real—to talk with us. Nothing happened for a good twenty minutes, at which point Barry said that he could sense the old man's presence right beside him.

The REM Pod screeched three times over the space of twenty seconds. As all our phones were either upstairs or set to airplane mode, we struggled to find a reason for the sudden increase in electromagnetic energy. Jason had placed the device in the middle of the basement, far away from any of the sources of EMF that we had identified during baselining.

"If you're here—and I know you're close—could you make the device go off again, please?" Barry asked. A minute passed without any response. Reading from the Ovilus, Jason asked whether the next name that came up—*Paula*—meant anything. The REM Pod lit up. Was this in direct response to Jason's question or a purely random electromagnetic spike?

"So does the name Paula mean anything to you?" he repeated, seeking clarification. The REM Pod went bananas, emitting a long, strangulated cry that lasted for a good thirty seconds, accompanied by a full array of flashing lights on top of the device. This indicated an electromagnetic field of significant strength.

I asked Barry if he knew a Paula. He shook his head no. From the corner of my eye, I was convinced that I could see a shadow dart from one corner of the room to another. I freely admit it could have been my eyes playing tricks, the product of jet lag and low light conditions, but then again . . .

We moved the REM Pod across to that same corner, and all backed away. Barry confided that the corner was one of the most uncomfortable spots in the entire basement for him. He hadn't given us the specific location until now because he had wanted to see what we picked up. The corner had been completely inert so far as our EMF meters had been concerned.

Our questioning became a little more specific. Was the spirit somebody who had worked here? What year had that been?

Had this person died in the substation, and if so, why had they remained behind after death?

Our session was interrupted by the regular arrival of trains pulling into the station overhead. The REM Pod stayed dark and silent, right up until Barry asked, "Do you mean us any harm?"

Electronic squealing and flashing lights suggested that the spirit did.

Staying polite, Barry tried to get the entity to elaborate. The REM Pod refused to cooperate once more, no matter what he asked. For the next quarter of an hour, our questions were all pointedly ignored. Getting somewhat exasperated, I asked the entity to switch on the lights again. Instantly, the REM Pod sprang to life but then went back to its usual sullen silence when further questions were asked.

I sighed. This was becoming frustrating. There were no identifiable sources of electromagnetic energy down in the basement to explain the sudden EMF spikes in what had turned out to be a remarkably well-shielded building, one with extremely thick concrete floors and walls that were also lead-lined. The arriving trains weren't the cause, as none of the energy bursts occurred when we heard the squeal of brakes up above us.

Our host hit upon the idea of picking up a K2 meter and asking the entity to approach him. Holding the EMF meter loosely in one hand, he moved toward the corner where I thought that I had seen the shadow figure and asked whether the spirit was willing to come and join him. As if in answer, the REM Pod screeched and flashed. Yet the K2 itself remained silent.

"Are you playing games with us?" I demanded. A knock came in response. A second knock sounded when I asked, "Are you still here with us?"

Linda suddenly began to feel cold. When Lesley asked aloud if this was being caused by the spirit, she was rewarded with the loudest click-knock we had heard all night. The odd noises had seemed to be moving around the room.

We tried in vain for the next half hour to establish some kind of contact, but our equipment remained maddeningly quiet. Whatever had been triggering it appeared to have gone. Even Barry felt that it was calm and peaceful down in the basement, and so reluctantly we decided to call it a night.

Stopping for one last cup of tea, Barry closed out by telling us about an experience he and a colleague had had in the building the year before. This man was an East Londoner of the old school, a former boxer, and not one to believe in ghosts or "all that rubbish."

As the two men sat upstairs, Barry told his fellow employee that he thought something was going to happen that night. No sooner had he spoken those words than they heard a door open and close downstairs on the ground floor.

"Somebody just came in," Barry's colleague said. Suppressing a smile, Barry just shook his head, knowing full well that nobody had entered the old power house. Not taking Barry's word for it, he got up and went to see for himself, searching high and low. Of course, the building was completely deserted.

Meeting up again after the search, the two men sat down in uncomfortable silence. Barry was sensing that their unseen visitor was about to leave and said as much. His colleague scoffed at the idea but changed his tune just a minute later when the exit door opened and slammed shut again, with no living person to account for it.

The boxer drank his tea in one big gulp, slammed the cup down, and left Barry alone in the building for the rest of the night!

On that note, we shook hands with Barry and thanked him for sharing some of the ghost lore of the London Underground with us and allowing us to investigate the unidentified entity that haunted the Victorian-era power house. As we drove back to our hotel to catch a few precious hours of sleep, I tried to figure out just what it was that had caused our instruments to behave so erratically down in that basement. Had we really been in contact with the building's resident ghost, or was there a far more mundane explanation for it all?

The truth is I will probably never know for sure. My mind was already looking ahead toward the rest of the day, when I would cross an item off my bucket list that I had desperately wanted to do for decades: move in with what was said to be the world's most violent poltergeist, the Black Monk of Pontefract.

CHAPTER 5

HUNTING THE BLACK MONK

Of the many different types of haunting that have been cataloged by paranormal researchers, arguably the most perplexing is that of the "noisy spirit," or as it is more commonly known, the poltergeist.

Poltergeist outbreaks tend to be relatively short in duration (lasting for months, sometimes a few years at most) and violent in nature. Objects are hurled across rooms; fires may break out without an apparent ignition source, only to quell themselves before burning the entire building down; mysterious pools of water appear and disappear, seemingly at random; and in the most extreme cases, physical injury is inflicted upon the poor soul that appears to be the focus of the poltergeist.

In the recorded annals of psychic phenomena, a handful of poltergeist cases stand out above the rest. They are considered to be so remarkable, so spectacular, and so downright bizarre, that they have attained legendary status among scholars of the paranormal.

The absolute king of them all has to be the Black Monk of Pontefract. This malevolent entity unleashed a reign of terror upon the innocent Pritchard family during the 1960s and 1970s, making a small, anonymous house in Pontefract, England, into a national sensation that had members of the media camping outside the property overnight in the hopes of catching the Black Monk in action.

My personal fascination with all things ghostly began when I was a young boy, haunting (pun intended) my local library in order to repeatedly devour every book on the shelves that talked about ghosts and hauntings. One of my favorites was a book called *Poltergeist!*, written by the late Colin Wilson. It was an in-depth analysis of the poltergeist phenomenon, offering up theories and covering some of the most famous cases on record. The book is still in print today, and I heartily recommend it.

The case that frightened me the most was of course that of the Black Monk, which gave me more than a few nightmares—but didn't stop me from reading further. Never in my wildest dreams did the younger me think that one day he would be moving into that very same house in Pontefract for a week of paranormal investigation that I would never forget.

Origins

The Pritchard family comprised Joe, Jean, their fifteen-year-old son, Phillip, and their twelve-year-old daughter, Diane. It is fair to say that the family had its share of tensions, something that is fairly common in poltergeist outbreaks, and their bond would be tested to its very limits by the events that began in the summer of 1966, when a strange chalky substance began to float down from just below the ceiling. The powder settled in a fine layer upon the furniture, the floor, and the heads of Phillip and his grandmother, who happened to be babysitting him at the time while the rest of the family were on holiday. Neighbors also witnessed the phenomenon, watching incredulously as the powder kept on falling from just below the ceiling.

The bell had just been rung for the first round of what would turn out to be an absolute nightmare for the Pritchards, one that people are still arguing about to this very day.

Unexplained pools of standing water came next, appearing all over the house and defying the ability of the local water board maintenance men to make them stop. Keys rained down from the chimney one morning, scaring the life out of poor Mrs. Pritchard. Green slime ran from the taps. Objects moved through the air, sometimes floating serenely, at other times flying as though hurled with immense force.

Disembodied footsteps sounded from rooms of the house that were completely empty. Drawers pulled themselves out and the cupboards rattled and shook, opening and closing of their own accord.

At first the phenomena seemed mostly pranksterish, even playful in nature, such as the time when a jug full of milk floated across the room and poured itself over the head of a visiting aunt. Yet things soon took on a darker turn, as the poltergeist began to show its true colors.

The family would come downstairs to find that photographs of themselves had been slashed with knives. Visitors began to sustain minor injuries, more frightening than harmful, such as pinches and slaps. The staircase became something to be feared, as the poltergeist soon developed a penchant for shoving people as they went up or down it. Fortunately, nobody broke any bones, but the intent seemed clear enough: this was the poltergeist's house, not the Pritchards', and they were to be its playthings so long as they chose to remain there.

The Coal Hole

One day, Joe Pritchard underwent a life-changing experience inside a small coal storage closet that was known as the "coal hole." In addition to their wages, many miners were paid in coal, just the thing to keep the fire going on those cold winter nights. We do not know exactly what happened to Joe inside the coal hole—it was a subject that he was extremely leery of talking about—but the rumors are that he was subjected to a brutal physical assault by the poltergeist, one that left him emotionally scarred and eager to move from 30 East Drive for good.

Jean was made of sterner stuff, however, and flatly refused to be chased out of her own home by a spirit, no matter how vicious it appeared to be. In an obvious attempt to break some of the poltergeist's hold over them, she and the family took to calling him "Fred." The British press had other ideas, and soon christened the poltergeist "Mr. Nobody" in one of the many newspaper articles that featured the Pritchards and their plight.

Despite several attempts to get rid of him by means of exorcism and blessing ceremonies, Fred laughed in the face of the clergy. This may have been partly because he was once one of them, for the entity behind it all was said to be the lingering spirit of a long-dead Cluniac monk. The story went that he had been executed after sexually assaulting a young girl, and his body was then tossed down a nearby well … supposedly on the ground that 30 East Drive now stood upon.

There are several problems with this story (no matter the crime, who would be stupid enough to poison something as useful as a well, for example?), but one thing is for certain: when Fred finally did put in appearance, he was wearing the hooded robes of a monk with a black mask beneath the cowl where his face should have been.

Things finally came to a head when Diane was attacked in front of her family, being dragged up the staircase by an invisible force that left clear strangulation marks upon the pale skin of her throat.

So many strange occurrences took place during the course of the initial haunting that they could fill a book of their own, and I encourage readers to seek out Colin Wilson's book to learn more about them.

As time passed, the ghostly activity finally began to wane but never entirely went away. The two children grew up and moved out, building lives of their own. Joe Pritchard collapsed and died on the bathroom floor upstairs at the top of the staircase. Still refusing to be chased out of her own home, Jean gamely soldiered on alone at 30 East Drive. According to those who knew her, she spent much of her time living in a state of anxiety.

When the Lights Went Out

Media interest in the case dissipated along with the phenomena, yet by all accounts the haunting never truly stopped. Jean finally gave up and moved out when a film about the case (*When the Lights Went Out*) was released in 2012, leaving the house empty and abandoned. At the time of writing in 2017, she is said to be living nearby and is quite happy to be rid of the house that brought her and her family so much misery.

One of the producers of *When the Lights Went Out* was Bil Bungay. The movie itself was shot primarily on soundstages, but the house used for the exterior shots was not 30 East Drive. When he heard that the real Black Monk House was up for sale, he snapped it up like a shot.

To this day, he still isn't sure whether it was one of his best or worst decisions.

With a background in advertising, Bil took a very active hand in promoting the movie. Buying 30 East Drive now provided him with an irresistible opportunity to do something truly unique: hold the premiere of his motion picture in the house on which the movie was based. For the lucky winners, it would be the chance to watch the movie first, possibly with Fred himself lurking around to watch it with them.

From the moment he first stepped foot inside the house, strange things began happening to Bil. His usually reliable phone died in his hand, its battery suffering a 75 percent drain in the space of a few heartbeats. Bil was a hardened skeptic and found most of the ghost stories circulating about Number 30 to be very hard to swallow. Yet as the strangeness mounted, even he was eventually forced to start believing in the impossible. Cleaning up after a documentary film crew late one night, Bil took the trash out to the dustbin and then went to close the double wrought iron gates. Making sure that they were properly secured, he placed a hefty chunk of concrete against them for good measure, just to make it harder for any would-be trespasser.

The author outside the infamous Black Monk House.

Bil turned away from the gate to see two of his companions just exiting the house, happy to be out of the place and ready to hit the road. When he turned back a few seconds later, he nearly had a heart attack—one of the gates had swung wide open. To make matters worse, it was the one that he had wedged shut with the chunk of concrete, which was now sitting off to one side of the driveway.

That's when he became a believer.

With the release of the movie, the house became increasingly popular again. People would come from far and wide just to ogle the "Pontefract ghost house." According to Carol Fieldhouse, who lived next door in the directly connected neighboring house, bangs, thuds, footsteps, and all manner of bizarre noises regularly came out of the empty Number 30 in the early hours of the morning, including the clear sound of a television set. Such phenomena regularly bled through into her own house as well, Carol told me; hardly a surprise, as ghosts are not known for respecting brick walls as boundaries.

Serial visits from the controversial TV show *Most Haunted* sealed the deal for 30 East Drive's reputation as one of the most paranormally active locations in the United Kingdom, not to mention putting the house firmly on my bucket list of must-investigate places. After doing a bit of legwork, I found out that Bil did allow overnight paranormal investigations there for a modest fee. I lived in America, however, and it was a long way to travel for a night in a haunted house, even one with as fearsome a reputation as 30 East Drive.

Nevertheless, I reached out to Bil and spent some time chatting with him via Skype. We hit it off immediately, and when he found out that I was a writer who wanted to investigate his haunted property and write about it, he excused himself to go and check his day planner.

"How would you like to move in there for five days and nights?" he asked me casually, practically knocking my socks off.

"I'd give my right arm for that," I told him, only halfway kidding.

"That's not necessary," Bil laughed. "No money required, in fact. I allow theoretical physicists to investigate the house for free. You can do it too. Just do good research and tell the true story when you come to write it. Deal?"

Oh, hell yes, it was a deal.

I was on cloud nine when I logged off Skype. This was the case of a lifetime, so far as I was concerned, and I immediately set about doing some online research. Eyewitness accounts coming out of 30 East Drive tended to fall into one of two camps, I noticed: either "nothing happened to us at all—this was a complete waste of time" or "this place crawls with paranormal activity—I can't believe what happened to us!" I very much hoped that the latter would turn out to be true for me when I moved in there the following summer.

The Team

One of the nice things about investigating an ordinary private residence is that is doesn't take too many people in order to cover the place effectively. Nevertheless, I wanted to pick and choose my team carefully. A small crew was in order, but they had to be experienced and trustworthy.

My first port of call was an easy one. Two of my most trusted investigators Stateside were Jason and Linda Fellon, two people whom I had spent countless hours with at haunted locations across the US. They also happen to be very good personal friends. When I phoned them up and explained the circumstances of my latest case, I really didn't expect them to be willing to fly thousands of miles across the Atlantic with me just to hunt for ghosts. I needn't have worried. They agreed on the spot, filling half my team roster instantly.

Charlie Stiffler was an emergency medical technician who had once worked with me at an ambulance company where I was a paramedic training chief. He had gotten into paranormal investigation after hearing some of my stories and had joined BCPRS, going through a smooth apprenticeship and graduating as a field investigator. He was willing to take a week away from his family in order to move into 30 East Drive and help me unravel its secrets.

Last but by no means least came Andrew Cooper. Andy was an experienced paranormal investigator from the UK. We knew one another due to a mutual interest in science fiction and had gone to conventions together in the past. He would travel the least amount of distance but put a great deal of effort into our five-day investigation. Every bit as importantly, he made a great cup of tea.

Jason, Linda, and I spent our first night in England investigating the London Underground station that you read about in the last chapter. Charlie and Andy were going to meet us in Pontefract. After a few precious hours of sleep, the three of us piled into our rental car and began the long drive north to Pontefract with Jason behind the wheel.

The sense of anticipation I felt is difficult to convey. Usually on long car journeys, I like to lose myself in the pages of a good book or a magazine, which tends to make the miles fly by. On the way to Pontefract, I wasn't able to concentrate on much of anything. I was too excited at the prospect of what the next five days might have in store for us.

I have investigated more than my fair share of historic old buildings, ranging from manor houses and castles all the way up to a sixteenth-century witches' prison. Many of them looked as though they ought to have been haunted, no matter whether they actually were or not. One of the things that struck me about the Chequerfield Estate in Pontefract was the sheer normality of it all. This was the same sort of English housing estate that I had grown up in, with kids running and playing in the street, people carrying shopping bags home from the store, and cars parked in rows along either side of the street.

It most certainly did not look like the sort of place where one might find one of Great Britain's most haunted houses.

"There it is," Jason said as we approached a roundabout (or traffic circle, for my American readers). The navigation system told us that we had reached our destination, and sure enough, the two-story brick house was directly in front of us. I hopped out and opened up the very same gate that had closed itself on Bil Bungay four years earlier, and we parked the rental car in the driveway, leaving our cases of equipment locked up inside it for now.

"So this is it." I could hardly believe that I was actually here, standing outside the place I had read so much about over the past thirty years. The garden was neat and tidy. Knocking on the front door, we were met by a friendly young fellow named Scott who was part of the local paranormal investigation team that took its name from the house: East Drive Paranormal.

We shook hands, and Scott immediately offered to make us a cup of tea. I jumped at the chance. Jet lag and the general fatigue that came from lack of sleep vanished in an instant, replaced by a surge of adrenaline-fueled excitement. This was it—the ghost hunter's holy grail.

The Black Monk House.

Heed the Warnings

The first warning signs that this was no ordinary house were the laminated notices that had been taped onto the outside of the kitchen door. I read them with mounting excitement.

IMPORTANT NOTICE! 30 East Drive has a strict NO OUIJA BOARDS rule, as we don't want to exacerbate the situation. Anyone found abusing this rule will be ejected from the property and blacklisted on our website.

"I guess the board stays in the car," Linda said, sounding just a little disappointed. I was too, but I couldn't say that I blamed Bil in the slightest. If even a fraction of the stories about this place were true, the Black Monk wasn't an entity we wanted to make angry at us.

Directly above the first sign was a second, which read,

By entering 30 East Drive you agree that you are person-ally liable for your own safety. The owner cannot be held responsible. If you are unhappy with this, you must leave the property now.

The three of us chatted with Scott for a while, listening eagerly to his personal experiences inside the house. He and his fellow members of East Drive Paranormal acted as caretakers for the house, cleaning it up in between investigations and generally keeping an eye on the place.

Charlie and Andy arrived soon afterward. No sooner had they been introduced to Scott than another man stepped into the kitchen, just walking in as if he owned the place—which in fact he did. Bil and I shook hands. It was good to meet in person finally. After a round of introductions had been made, he asked whether we would like the grand tour.

Would we *ever*.

On a side note, I am a keen student of human behavior, as most paramedics are: whenever I meet somebody new, I make a point of watching them closely and reading their body language as much as I possibly can. From the moment he had stepped into the house, Bil reminded me of a soldier in a combat zone. His head was on a swivel, constantly looking around him as though scanning for potential threats. Bil's posture was tense, further cementing my belief that he felt less than comfortable in this environment.

"Hello, Fred! It's me again—Bil. I don't mean you any harm!" he called out, stepping slowly and carefully into the hallway that led off from the kitchen. His tone was friendly, yet it also held a definite undercurrent of nervousness.

He led us upstairs first. Although it looked like any other staircase in an ordinary English house, my mind kept reminding me that I was climbing the very same steps up that Diane Pritchard had been dragged up by the Black Monk decades ago, kicking and choking helplessly in the grip of that unseen entity.

A door at the top of the stairs stood open. Bil explained that this was the bathroom in which Joe Pritchard had died. I stuck my head inside. It was decorated primarily with pink and white tiles in an attempt to be cheery, but I found it to be rather sinister—then again, I wondered, would you still feel that way if you didn't know its history?

Next came Phillip's room. *Most Haunted* had captured some incredible video footage in the room of several white balls moving around the carpet, seemingly of their own volition. The room looked very much as it must have during the 1960s and 1970s, complete with a single bed, an old portable TV set, and posters of the Beatles and the Osmond Family brightening up the walls.

The downstairs hallway at 30 East Drive,
fifteen minutes after our arrival.

The master bedroom had of course belonged to Mr. and Mrs. Pritchard. It had a large double bed and several pieces of bedroom furniture, including a rather creepy-looking doll named Victoria. During the initial poltergeist outbreak, Joe and Jean had spent many nights cowering in bed, listening to the entity that had invaded their home as it stomped around the house into the wee hours of the morning. Much of the current wave of paranormal activity was also said to take place in this room, and I was looking forward to seeing just what results we would get in here.

The smallest bedroom had belonged to Diane. It was full of toys suitable for a much younger child, which Bil said were often used as control objects by visiting investigators. Above the single bed hung a painting of a crying child, which further contributed to the atmosphere of gloom and doom that seemed to pervade the entire upper floor. Bil pointed up to the Styrofoam-tiled ceiling, which was covered in scratches and scuff marks.

"Diane is supposed to have been levitated up to the ceiling by the poltergeist, and those are said to be scratch marks she made in a panic," he told us. Personally, I was skeptical of this, but it did make for a great story.

We made sure to take reference photographs as we went, documenting the layout of each room and the landing. This would turn out to be a very smart move on our part later that same day. I paused at the foot of the stairs to shoot pictures of the staircase itself and the downstairs hallway. An old mirror hung on the wall directly facing the stairs; it stood out in my memory because I remembered seeing it on *Most Haunted*.

Leading the way from the hallway into the living room, Bil explained that he had tried to give the house as much of a 1960s/1970s feel as he possibly could. This had involved touring the local charity shops for knickknacks from that time period, which included period-specific paintings, ornaments, and, best of all, a set of genuine Betamax video tapes.

The living room was directly connected to a small dining room and kitchen by a set of double doors. I noticed that there were bolts on the doors, which I found to be rather unusual. Bil said that during her time living alone at 30 East Drive, Jean

Pritchard had been so uneasy that she had bolted the doors shut in a vain attempt to keep Fred at bay. It was the first time I had ever heard of somebody trying to lock a ghost out of the room.

The dining room was compact but comfortable. It was furnished with a piano, an easy chair, and a small table, and opened out onto the kitchen. Just beyond the front door through which we had entered was a downstairs toilet. Next to that sat the infamous coal hole in which Joe Pritchard had experienced his violent showdown with Fred. Looking inside, I saw that it was dirty and covered in grime, smelling faintly of damp and old brick.

"This is our evidence room," Bil said, indicating a doorway at the end of the short hall. What might once have been a laundry room or scullery was now festooned from floor to ceiling with laminated maps, photographs, and newspaper articles covering every aspect of the Black Monk haunting, many of them gathered by paranormal investigators. Several contained dark, mysterious figures, whereas others had captured unusual light phenomena that went far above and beyond the usual dust-induced "orb" photos that are such a staple in the field of paranormal tourism.

"Wow." Jason let out a low whistle. "I'm gonna have to spend some time studying all this stuff."

"Be my guest," Bil said, "but right now I think it's time for lunch, don't you?"

So great was our excitement at finally getting to set foot inside the Black Monk House that we had all forgotten just how hungry we were. A pub lunch was quickly agreed upon. Before Bil locked up the house, I excused myself for a second and dashed upstairs. I had extracted a digital voice recorder from my equipment bag for just this purpose, because I had a bad case of FOMO—fear of missing out—and wanted a record of what was happening at 30 East Drive in our absence.

I set the recorder down on the upstairs landing and started it running.

"See you later, Fred," Bil called cheerily over his shoulder before locking the front door behind us. He drove us to the nearest pub, where he kindly treated me to a traditional English roast dinner and a pint of Coke (we don't permit alcohol on our investigations). We talked about the house and Bil's involvement with it and kicked around a few theories about why it seemed to be so paranormally active.

Seven Years' Bad Luck

We were gone for no more than an hour. It was still early afternoon when we arrived back at Number 30, and for the second time I was struck by just how normal the house appeared from the outside. If one didn't know of its haunted history, it would be easy to walk past without giving it so much as a second glance.

Bil unlocked the front door and went inside, once again saying hello to Fred. If I had been harboring any thoughts about how unusual it was to greet a seemingly empty house, they were dispelled when Bil walked through the kitchen and into the hallway. I was right on his heels and was startled when he suddenly stopped dead in his tracks and let out a surprised gasp.

The wall-mounted mirror that had been hanging at the foot of the stairs was now lying on the carpeted floor, its glass split in half by a long crack. I swore softly under my breath. Bil reached out to examine the damage, but I stopped him before he could touch it. "Photographs first," I explained. We needed to treat this like a crime scene, documenting it from every angle before disturbing anything.

Once we had taken a bunch of pictures, Bil picked up the mirror cautiously and examined it. It had hung from a thick length of twine. The nail was still in place, but the string itself had snapped in two, as though it had been yanked forcefully from the wall and then dropped.

On taking a closer look at the snapped twine, I found it to be surprisingly thick and strong. The mirror had hung in that same spot for years. Now, within less than an hour of my team and me first setting foot inside 30 East Drive, what were the odds that it would decide to spontaneously snap?

"Looks like Fred's way of welcoming you to the house," Bil said.

Thrilled as I was to finally be here at the Black Monk House, I hadn't quite taken leave of my senses—particularly the sense of healthy skepticism that I had spent years cultivating. Although the timing of it might be one hell of a coincidence, I knew that jumping to the conclusion that Fred had been the one responsible for breaking the mirror in our absence would have been premature.

What we came back to after going to lunch.
Fred's idea of a warm welcome?

Not wanting to appear rude in front of Bil, we waited for him to leave before voicing the obvious explanation. "Somebody with a spare key could have been here while we were getting lunch," Linda pointed out. "Sneaked in and then smashed the mirror."

"Bil might not know anything about it," added Jason, "but maybe a friend of his thinks that the publicity could be a good thing and is trying to help Bil out... especially if they heard that a writer was moving into the house for a week."

In all my conversations with Bil, I had gotten the distinct impression that he was a man of integrity. He was showing a lot of trust by giving a virtual stranger the keys to his property. But not everybody was as honest, and fraud is one of the first things a paranormal investigator needs to consider, especially in high-profile cases such as this one.

Now seemed like the ideal time to tell the team about the digital voice recorder I had surreptitiously placed at the top of the stairs before leaving for the pub. Any flesh-and-blood intruder should have been picked up on the audio recording, all being well. Retrieving the recorder from its hiding place, I brought it back downstairs and hooked it up to an external speaker.

The single file on the device ran for a little over an hour. I started from the beginning. We all gathered around for a listen. There was the sound of my heavy footsteps thudding down the staircase, the distant noises of our team chatting excitedly, and then the sound of the front door closing.

We strained our ears, listening to the sounds of an empty house. The recorder was fairly sensitive and would occasionally pick up the sound of a car passing by outside. I waited on tenterhooks, fully expecting to hear the creak of a door opening at any moment, followed by the furtive footsteps of a stealthy intruder.

They never came.

Even though we knew it would happen sooner or later, the crash startled us all.

"That's the mirror hitting the ground," Charlie said, stating the obvious.

I ran the file back two minutes and played it again, really listening and trying to pick out the sound of a door opening or a creaking floorboard; yet there were no other sounds, either before the crash or afterward.

We had been through every room in the house prior to leaving, checking everything down to the cupboard under the stairs and the water heater closet in Phillip's bedroom. There had been no places where somebody could have hidden, and besides, the recorder hadn't picked up the sound of a door closing after the crash either. Just to rule out the "hidden accomplice" theory, we searched the house from top to bottom again, proving that it was still completely empty.

But we weren't quite done yet. What if there had indeed been an intruder, one whose movements were so stealthy that they hadn't been detected on our voice recorder? I for one found the idea hard to believe (the particular model of recorder that I use picks up almost anything audible) but just to test the theory, we set the device back at the top of the stairs and invited Jason, arguably the lightest member of our group, to enter the house from outside and try to replicate the feat.

Jason spent five minutes just opening the door, turning the handle centimeter by painstaking centimeter. Once he was inside, he tiptoed slowly and quietly through the kitchen and into the hallway. When he reached the foot of the stairs, we played the recording back. Despite his very best efforts, the sound of the door creaking on its hinges could be heard very clearly, and his footsteps could be made out as he got within a few feet of where the mirror had formerly hung.

We repeated the experiment a few more times with other investigators taking their turns to try to beat the recording, but each time the result was the same: clear, audible evidence on playback.

I found myself agreeing with Bil: Fred had rolled out the welcome mat (or in this case, the welcome mirror) for us. What other surprises did he have in store?

Scratched

Our first night passed quietly. After baselining each room in order to identify areas of high EMF caused by the electrical appliances, we spent much of the evening just settling in and getting used to the natural rhythms of the house. We quickly learned to identify the sounds caused by the house contracting at night, as parts of it had expanded during the heat of the July day and returned to normal after cooling off.

We conducted the usual series of EVP experiments, rotating from room to room and calling out to whatever entities might be present. EMF levels remained flat. Nothing turned up on our video or audio evidence review the following morning. The house just seemed…normal.

Despite the lack of paranormal activity, the Black Monk House was nevertheless beginning to creep me out. I didn't mention it to any of my companions, primarily because I didn't want to seem weird, but something about the place was setting my nerves on edge.

Undoubtedly, a large part of my discomfort, if not all of it, was purely psychological in nature. Having read about the case since childhood, I was still adjusting to the fact that I was really here, sitting in the same living room and kitchen in which the Pritchards had been mercilessly tormented by the Black Monk all those years ago. It was one thing to read about it in the pages of a book or to see it dramatized on a movie screen, but actually living inside the same space felt a little surreal.

I am a child of the seventies, and the interior of 30 East Drive was like a time machine that took me straight back to those days. It reminded me of my grandmother's house, all the way down to the decor and furnishings; the house filled me with a sense of familiarity that was downright unnerving, a low-grade level of constant discomfort that I had never felt in any of the other haunted locations that I had investigated over the years. The house was hitting me very close to home, and I wasn't at all sure that the explanation was necessarily a paranormal one.

One man who wasn't remotely put off by his surroundings was Charlie. He spent a hefty amount of time sleeping off his jet lag, napping by turns on the living room couch and all the upstairs bedrooms. Although we gave him a hard time about it, I actually found the idea of an investigator getting a lot of sleep to be a valuable one; sleep is by its very definition an altered state of consciousness, and it has been theorized that the dead can sometimes use the medium of dreaming to communicate with us. Given that this was the Black Monk House, I was half expecting

Charlie to wake up screaming after a brain-bender of a night-mare, but that never came to pass.

Instead, the entity decided to get physical with him. Charlie was standing at the kitchen sink washing up, just minding his own business. The rest of us were hanging out in the dining room or living room, making notes and reviewing evidence.

"Hey guys," he called out suddenly, "Somebody's grabbing my ankles."

He shuffled backward awkwardly, fighting to keep his balance. We have a strict policy in BCPRS of never joking about phenomena, so everybody came running. Charlie described feeling a pair of hands grabbing him firmly by the ankles and trying to pull him off balance.

"Your ankles seem all right," I said, peering at the pale white flesh. "No red marks or anything like that."

"Now my back is burning up." He was beginning to sound a little concerned. Andy lifted up Charlie's shirt and exposed the skin. A series of three angry red scratches ran in parallel across his lower back, running from high up on the right side toward the bottom left. Each scratch was a good ten inches in length.

I let out a low whistle. "Somebody got you good, Charlie."

We took photos of Charlie's back from all angles, some of them using a thermal camera. Some members of the paranormal research community believe that when it comes to scratches, the number three is of great significance, chosen specifically to mock the Holy Trinity, and claim that three scratches are an indicator of a demonic or inhuman entity. While this doesn't fit with my personal belief system as an agnostic, it is an opinion that is held by a number of clergy members whose work I hold in high regard, so I would never dismiss it out of hand.

Is it possible that Charlie chose to fake this, scratching his own back when nobody was looking? Absolutely. This is always something that must be considered when paranormal activity occurs. Yet Charlie has worked on a number of cases during his time as a BCPRS investigator, and not once have we had even the slightest reason to question his integrity. Unless we are given cause to do differently, we give our investigators the benefit of the doubt when things such as this happen.

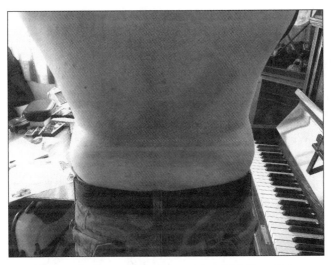

Charlie's back, courtesy of the spirits of 30 East Drive.

Minor physical injuries were commonplace during the original haunting, and a number of visitors have reported being similarly scratched on various parts of their body.

The Black Monk, it appeared, was upping the ante on us.

The Royal Air Force Drops In

We assumed that Charlie's scratches were the first sign of bigger things to come, but as it turned out, we were mistaken on that particular score.

The next few days were quiet and broody inside the house. We pulled out all the stops trying to stimulate the entity to come out and engage with us, including taking turns being locked in the coal hole (that one got my heart pounding, let me tell you) and wheedling, coaxing, and sometimes outright provoking it. All to no avail.

30 East Drive stubbornly refused to cooperate.

As the silence dragged on, our collective frustration mounted. We added some fresh blood into the mix by inviting our friends from East Drive Paranormal to join us; despite the pleasure of their company, the Black Monk was nowhere to be found.

One bright spot was a flying visit from my younger brother, Matt. We rarely get the chance to see one another, mainly due to the fact that I live in the United States and he travels the globe with the Royal Air Force. Although he won't tell you himself, Matt is one hell of a soldier, the sort of man who knows how to keep a cool head in a crisis. Most importantly, he doesn't scare easily.

After we met for breakfast and a long-overdue chat, I asked Matt if he'd like to come and visit the home of what some have called the world's most violent poltergeist. He was a little reluctant at first, but after some prodding from his wife and kids, soon accepted the challenge.

Matt parked his car a little way down the street and followed me up the path to Number 30. After introducing himself to my fellow investigators, I gave him a similar tour to the one that Bil had given us when we had first arrived. It was interesting to watch Matt's body language as he went tentatively from room to room. He appeared hyperalert and unsettled, which are both very out of character for him. All in all, he spent less than ten minutes inside the house, pausing only to take a few photos before heading out again.

My brother and I have very different personalities. I tend to be the pie-in-the-sky creative type, whereas Matt is the down-to-earth realist. Perhaps that's why I found his parting comment to be a little on the strange side.

"There's something about that house," he said, turning around to look at the warning signs that Bil had posted on the inner door. "Something evil. How long are you staying again?"

"Five days in all," I told him.

"Rather you than me, mate." With those words, Matt went back to his everyday life of getting shot at for a living, which scared him less than the prospect of spending the night at 30 East Drive.

Voices

Our investigation was beginning to wind down. Just as we had given up our hopes of there being more paranormal activity, we learned that 30 East Drive had saved up one final parting shot for us.

Local investigators Andy Evans and Nick Hawkins dropped by to pay us a visit. Andy and Nick had spent many hours investigating the house shortly after the resurgence of national interest that was caused by the release of *When the Lights Went Out*. They had captured some incredible photographs, many of which adorned the walls of Bil's evidence room, including one of a dark, shadowy figure at the top of the stairs that I found to be particularly chilling.

Both men had written their own books about the house but hadn't been back inside in quite some time. I had wanted to sit down with them to conduct an interview, which turned out to be very enlightening. Once it was over, they kindly offered to set up an EVP session with us. We gathered around the small dining room table while our visitors set up their equipment, one of which was a spirit box–type device that Andy called "the Parabula."

The session began slowly, with a great deal of gibberish coming through the external speakers that were being used. We waited patiently and continued to ask questions, letting Andy and Nick do most of the talking. It's important for me to make clear that at no point did either of them say my name.

A few minutes in, a male voice suddenly piped up and said, "Richard Estep."

I was astonished. "Did that just say my name?"

Based upon the nods I was getting from all around the table, I was guessing that everybody else had heard the same thing I just did.

I asked Andy to play it back. Lo and behold, there it was again: "Richard Estep."

One thing that had to be taken into consideration was the possibility of audio pareidolia—the tendency of our brains to hear meaningful words in what is really just random noise. The mind likes to do the same things with visual images, the most common example of which is the man in the moon. Audio pareidolia is a common problem with EVP recordings. Had something really just spoken my name through the speaker, or were our minds simply fooling us into thinking that?

To this day, I'm not entirely sure either way. I have heard some truly compelling voice phenomena over the years, and even then I am often reluctant to truly nail my colors to the mast and declare them to be paranormal in origin.

As we shook hands with Andy and Nick and began to pack our equipment into the back of our rental car, I couldn't quite shake the feeling that 30 East Drive wasn't quite done with me yet. I had no idea at the time that I would be back again less than a year later for a second round.

The Storm Breaks

We departed Pontefract on Friday morning. Unbeknownst to me, new tenants moved in on the following Monday. Nick Groff and Katrina Weidman were spending a few days there, filming a special episode of their TV show *Paranormal Lockdown*.

I ran into Nick and Katrina at Dragon Con in Atlanta just one month later. We chatted about 30 East Drive, and I mentioned that while our stay had been interesting, it hadn't quite been the storm of ghostly activity that I had anticipated.

"You must have stirred it all up for us, because that place was insane!" Nick grinned. He couldn't give me much in the way of specifics, as the episode wouldn't air until Halloween, but promised me that some of the evidence they gathered would blow my mind.

When I finally sat down to watch the episode, I was indeed greatly impressed with some of their findings. One thing that struck me was the fact that during our investigation, the most impressive activity—the mirror, Charlie's scratches—happened very early on. During Nick and Katrina's stay, the activity seemed to start slowly and build.

Perhaps the most amazing piece of evidence they captured was video footage of what seems to be a full-body apparition, recorded on video as it moved past the living room door at a very brisk pace, heading toward the wall on which the broken mirror had once hung. This was the same glass door through which the shadowy figure of Fred had once peered in at the terrified Pritchard family.

Nick and Katrina also captured mysterious black shapes shooting across the floor between the living room and kitchen doorway. When I broached the subject with Carol, who lives next door to Number 30, she told me in a very matter-of-fact way that she had seen the same dark anomalies in her own house, which experiences a lot of bleed-over phenomena from its famous neighbor.

Back for More

In February of the following year, I took a night away from investigating the Hostel at 39 De Grey Street and made the one-hour drive from Hull to Pontefract. With me were fellow investigator Lesley and, for the first hour of the evening, a handful of friends from East Drive Paranormal.

We drove through torrential rain, and it was close to midnight when we arrived outside the Black Monk House. When we got inside, Lesley—who had never been to the house before—immediately said that the atmosphere felt heavy and oppressive. I generally don't pick up on things like that myself, but this time even I could feel it. Something about the house felt fundamentally wrong, although I couldn't put my finger on what exactly it was.

Not long after getting a quick tour, Lesley said that the atmosphere was now feeling very uncomfortable and made a run for the bathroom, where she began to retch and vomit. When she emerged a few minutes later, looking pale and slightly the worse for wear, I asked her why she had thrown up. She reiterated her feelings about the atmosphere, but also admitted that it could possibly be a simple case of mild food poisoning coupled with a late-night car journey.

A team from Manchester was packing up and getting ready to head home. They told us that the house had been somewhat active that night, but they hadn't gotten anything spectacular. By the time we had 30 East Drive all to ourselves, the heavy rain had eased off considerably.

We spent the night conducting EVP sessions in every room of the house. While Lesley and I were sitting at the top of the staircase next to the old wooden clock, we heard a gentle clatter coming from somewhere downstairs. We headed back down to try to determine the cause, but it took us a few moments to figure out exactly what had caused the sound: my cell phone, which I had left sitting on top of a small table in the living room, had slid roughly twelve inches across the table's surface, coming to rest somewhere in the middle.

I tried to come up with a simple explanation, but none sprang to mind. The phone had been left flat, not at an angle, so it would not have been possible for it to simply slide across the tabletop without some sort of push. Nobody else was in the house, so the only culprit left was . . . Fred.

Try as we might, however, we couldn't coax the Black Monk to put in an appearance. Somewhere around four o'clock in the morning, just as Lesley and I were beginning to doze off in armchairs, we began to glimpse flashes of light coming from the kitchen and dining room area. Each flash was only a split-second long, but see them we most definitely did. At first I thought they might be car headlights, but that theory was proven false when we paid a little more attention and verified that no cars were passing by outside at the time of each flash. There must have been five or six of them in total, separated out over the course of a couple of hours.

The sun still hadn't risen by six o'clock, and the flashes were now spaced further and further apart. These light anomalies seemed to originate inside the house, rather than being reflected in from the street outside, and try as we might, we could find no explanation for them. The five of us had spent many hours sitting awake all through the night during our five-day investigation the year before and hadn't seen any light phenomena to match this. To this day, I still don't have a solid explanation for the flashes, but I have heard similar stories from other visitors to 30 East Drive, so at the very least I am in good company.

At the time of writing, the Black Monk House remains paranormally active. Visitors continue to flock to the place, drawn by the fascinating tale of what may well be the most violent poltergeist outbreak ever recorded. I remain a keen observer of the case, corresponding regularly with Bil and some of the visiting investigators. To tell you the truth, I can't quite shake the feeling that I haven't yet spent my last night hunting for the Black

Monk of Pontefract. In spite of the fact that it lies thousands of miles away from where I live, 30 East Drive still feels like unfinished business to me.

Don't get too comfortable, Fred. One day I'll be back on your trail...

CHAPTER 6

THE HAUNTED MANSION

I have been fortunate enough to investigate some truly incredible locations over the course of the past twenty-two years, from haunted hospitals to insane asylums, the former home of a prolific serial killer to an ancient prison for witches, and abandoned ruins to desecrated churches. I have spent nights in all of these and many more in my almost obsessive quest to investigate claims of paranormal activity.

Yet none of them quite compares to the grandeur and beauty of Woodchester Mansion.

We had to drive halfway across the United Kingdom in order to get there, which was no mean feat considering just how tired we all were from having investigated all through the night before, then finally falling into our hotel bed before the sun came up for a few precious hours of sleep. We were back on the road before noon, heading for the picturesque village of Woodchester, which is situated on the edge of a large park that bears the same name.

William Leigh came from a wealthy mercantile family, having inherited a considerable sum of money from his father upon his passing. Leigh was a devout Catholic, and after he purchased the Woodchester estate, he immediately set about building a church, monastery, and above all else a great mansion, which was to stand on the site of a former mansion named Spring Park. Whether this was for religious purposes (the chapel at Woodchester is particularly grand) or in some way attributable to his involvement in Freemasonry, historians are not entirely sure.

Although Leigh and the architects both knew that the proposed great house would be an expensive proposition, neither of them suspected just how gargantuan a project it would turn out to be.

Building Woodchester Mansion was a chaotic affair, plagued by funding difficulties and labor issues. The wing that would house the servants went up first, situated on the north end of the structure. Considering the proposed size of the place, Leigh employed a workforce that was surprisingly small. Using primarily limestone that had been quarried locally and carted to the site, the various parts of the mansion slowly went up one block at a time.

Some twenty years after the builders had first broken ground, William Leigh died. His mansion was still not finished. A number of workers are said to have died during the lengthy construction process in a series of accidents, and there are even darker rumors of a stonemason's murder having taken place there.

The estate subsequently passed to William Leigh's son Willie, who lacked his father's emotional attachment to the uncompleted stone mansion. Taking stock of the situation, Willie commissioned professional estimates regarding how much money it would take to finish the mansion and to get it up and running. The completion costs ran to thousands of pounds, and the projected annual maintenance costs ran to similar heights. To make matters worse, it would even cost far too much to demolish the structure and do something else with the land upon which it had stood.

Approaching the Woodchester Mansion,
abandoned by its builders midconstruction.

Small wonder, then, that Willie Leigh chose to pull the plug. He would settle for living in a home known as the "Cottage" elsewhere on the estate, situated up on a hill and looking down on the mansion. Work on his father's great stone house was never completed. Woodchester Mansion remains unfinished to this day.

Numerous plans have been floated down through the years in order to allow the grand old house to fulfill some kind of greater purpose. A hospital for the mentally ill was proposed, as was a house of worship and a suite of offices. None of it ever quite came to fruition. The entire estate was used for the purpose of training soldiers during the Second World War.

As time wore on and Woodchester changed hands, the outdoor elements were less than kind, leaving the building in something of a run-down state. Fortunately, it is now in the care of the Woodchester Mansion Trust, which takes great care of the place and also allows the public to visit and experience the place for themselves. Among other things, it serves as a sanctuary where several endangered species of bats are able to rear their young while academics study their lives and behavior patterns.

The Woman in White

Ghost stories abound at Woodchester, and as with so many historic haunted locations, it is difficult to separate fact from folklore in some cases. One particularly intriguing story holds that the construction workers all simply downed tools and fled the mansion one day in 1886, never to return. Was this simply because the money ran out, or did something scare them off? As Association for the Scientific Study of Anomalous Phenomena (ASSAP) investigator Wendy Milner points out in her article A HAUNTED MANSION?, why would builders abandon their tools and equipment if they were knowingly leaving the construction site for the last time?

The apparition of a black dog has been reported from inside the gothic structure. In British folklore, the creature (often known as the "shuck" or "shag") is said to herald the death of either the unfortunate eyewitness or of somebody who has close ties to the area. Not to be outdone by its canine rival, a phantom black cat is occasionally seen in the area as well.

The woodland surrounding the mansion itself is said to be haunted by that most English of ghosts, a headless horseman, which some believe to be the apparition of Sir Rupert de Lansigny, a former owner of Woodchester Park. One wonders whether he talks to the ghostly Roman centurion who has also been spotted making his rounds in the area, or the spirit of the unfortunate gamekeeper who was said to have been ripped apart by his own vicious hunting dogs.

I had first learned about the place from the TV show *Most Haunted*, whose team conducted a live overnight ghost hunt there back in 2003 on the summer solstice. The presenters report having encountered a strange mist inside the building on their arrival during the middle of the day. Yet they were not the only TV production to visit Woodchester, or even the first; that title belongs to the makers of an American show called *The Scariest Places on Earth*, whose crew went there two years earlier in 2001. As recounted by Wendy Milner, the producers received the shock of their lives when the mansion rang out to the sound of many violent, pounding blows, so forceful that they feared the structure was coming down all around them.

One of the very first paranormal investigations carried out at Woodchester was a joint venture between ASSAP and the Ghost Club. As the investigators were driving down the long and winding track toward the mansion, they distinctly saw the figure of a lady wearing a long white dress standing in one of the windows overlooking their route. Eyewitness descriptions placed her somewhere in her twenties.

Due to the joint nature of the event, investigators from both sides simply assumed that the woman in white was a member of the other organization and at first gave very little thought to her presence. It was only when they entered the deserted mansion and realized that they were in fact the very first people to arrive that the truth began to dawn on them.

Rushing upstairs, the investigators set about identifying the window through which the mysterious woman had been seen. Identify it they did, but one can only imagine their surprise when they found that there was no floor beneath the window on which the woman could possibly have been standing.

The Woodchester Mansion had revealed its first apparition.

In the kitchens once hung a grand clock. During another ghost hunt conducted at Woodchester, it was seen to have changed the time on no less than three occasions; no big deal, you might think, until you learn that the clock no longer worked due to problems with the mechanism, which had almost completely corroded away. The mansion's bell, located high up in a locked bell tower that is completely inaccessible without possession of the keys, was heard to ring, and other loud bangs echoed through the empty corridors.

Haunted Hallways

Walking through the mansion corridors was something of a surreal experience. Even in its incomplete state, Woodchester Mansion is beautifully crafted; I couldn't help but be reminded of Hogwarts, the school of magic that is the setting for the Harry

Potter movies. Every so often we would come upon a little wooden gate. Our guide had warned us about these shortly after we had first arrived: they were quite literally doorways to no-where, steep drop-offs that could send the unwary visitor walking into empty air before crashing to their death on the stone floor far below.

During the Victorian era, it was a fairly common superstition for workmen to leave one of their boots behind in the roof of a building in order to ward off evil forces. The men who built Woodchester Mansion seem to have been believers, because there is indeed a single workman's boot still lodged in the rafters to this very day.

We made our way into a room known as the mortuary, which may seem an odd thing for an unfinished Victorian-era mansion to have. This storage area for the bodies of the dead dates back to the Second World War, when American and Canadian soldiers were using the place as a training ground in preparation to storm Hitler's Fortress Europe. Key to this training effort was the series of lakes that ran throughout Woodchester Park.

One of the training exercises went tragically wrong when the pontoon bridge that the soldiers had constructed in order to span the lake suddenly collapsed, possibly due to the additional weight of tanks and heavy artillery pieces, dumping the astonished soldiers into the icy cold water. Weighed down with weapon, boots, uniform, and full fighting kit, many of the men never stood a chance; an unknown number of them drowned before their comrades could rescue them from the lake.

The mortuary is so named because it is where the corpses of those unfortunate fighting men were stored prior to their being repatriated to the United States and to Canada for burial on their home soil. The room itself was designed to be a game larder, the equivalent of a modern-day walk-in refrigerator. It sits directly atop a 6,000-gallon water tank, which collects rainwater from the roof. A series of vents draw in air from outside and allow it to pass across the surface of the water, cooling the room down considerably. No wonder the three of us were shivering, even at the tail end of a hot July day!

Those same lakes were also the scene of a most unusual ghost sighting, the appearance of a coffin floating in the air above one of them. Legend has it that a local monk committed suicide by drowning in the lake and that the phantom coffin belongs to him. Just how much of the tale is true and how much can be put down to folklore is difficult to say.

Along with our friends from Haunted Happenings, a paranormal events company, we were to be given access to almost every area of the mansion that night. I could hardly wait to get started.

The chapel was beautiful though somewhat marred by the fact that the mansion's large menagerie of bats loved to use the ornate stonework as their own personal toilet. We eyed the darkness of the ceiling warily, expecting to be targeted with little white bomblets at any moment. Fortunately, the poop-storm never materialized, and we escaped the chapel unscathed.

Although I can't speak for Jason and Linda, the part of the investigation that I was most looking forward to was the basement. After all, who wouldn't be thrilled at the idea of experimenting in the cellar of a lonely stone mansion in the middle of a completely isolated woodland clearing? It was like an episode of *Scooby-Doo* come to life—and another item to check off on my paranormal investigator's bucket list!

Eagerly, we filed down into the cellar. The three of us weren't alone. A significant number of other would-be investigators were already clustered around down there, roughly fifteen of them. As the night wore on, we resolved to come back and check out the cellar on our own, but first we were starting out as a group. I saw this as very much a double-edged sword: on the one hand, just think of the potential paranormal activity that all of our combined energy could produce! But on the other, there was a greatly increased likelihood of rustling, shuffling, coughing, and other contamination of our audio data to be reckoned with. We had no real choice but to look on the bright side and see how things went.

We weren't to be disappointed.

Bartholomew

Lining up on either side of the corridor, we all stood facing one another with our backs to several stone arches, each of which led into empty rooms of various descriptions. We knew that the rooms were empty because I'd taken the liberty of sticking my head into each one and running the beam of my flashlight around. Nothing moved down there except for the occasional nervous mutter or chuckle from one of our companions.

One of those present that night was a medium named Sandra, who claimed to have made connections with two spirits that she said were down there in the cellar with us. She described the first as a monk-like male figure wearing a floor-length hooded robe. Although she couldn't see any crosses, rosaries, or other religious iconography, Sandra said that the figure was holding his hands in front of him, the fingers interlaced in the manner of a man at prayer.

Jason and I exchanged grins and a look that said, *Are we back at 30 East Drive, Pontefract, again?* We had spent a week searching for the infamous Black Monk, and the first entity we ran into at Woodchester Mansion met that description perfectly.

"He has been walking in and out of this room since we got here," Sandra explained. She gestured off toward her left. "Off on this side, I'm communicating with a spirit who tells me that his name is Bartholomew Gilbert. He says that he is forty-five years old and is very finely dressed in the manner of a Royalist."

Royalist is a term that harkens back to the English Civil War of 1642 and is often used interchangeably with the word *Cavalier.* The war was fought between followers of the Crown (the Royalists) and those who believed in rule by Parliament, known as Roundheads. The stereotypical Royalist would look like a foppish dandy; a good example might be the character of Nearly Headless Nick from the Harry Potter books and films. One of the many apparitions that have been reported at Woodchester is that of a Civil War–era horsemen, seen riding up the long driveway.

Sandra filled us in on Bartholomew Gilbert's life story. She said that he had been shot with several musket balls and had tried to make his way back to the place where Woodchester Mansion now stood, in the company of five of his comrades. She believed that he was most active in the area that had once been the wine cellar, which was just behind her. She went on to tell us that the back of his head was missing, presumably where one of the musket balls had struck him.

Having been to the mansion several times, Sandra had never encountered a spirit like Bartholomew before. He had never made it back to the mansion before succumbing to his wounds, she said, and she suspected that this was the reason why his energy was somehow being drawn back to this piece of land.

Our guide asked Sandra if she would please talk with Bartholomew and ask him to interact with us in some way during the course of the evening. She agreed that she would do so, not knowing what the consequences of that request would actually turn out to be.

"Bartholomew," she began, "could you please come forward—"

Before she could finish, Sandra was interrupted by the sound of a female visitor exclaiming that something had just touched her in the center of her back. "It felt as if I was being stroked through my cardigan," the woman explained, searching for the proper words to describe the eerie sensation.

"Please come forward, Bartholomew," Sandra continued, "There's no need to fear us. We're all on the same side as you: the side of the king…"

I stifled a laugh, looking at Linda and Jason. My friends from the United States definitely didn't qualify as being on "the side of the king," the rebellious colonials!

Sandra asked Bartholomew to walk around us and make a sound, and to make physical contact with one of us again. She rapped three times on the stone wall, and we were rewarded with a single answering tap in return.

Now things were getting interesting.

During the *Most Haunted Live* broadcast, presenters claimed to have encountered the spirit of an adult male, roughly three feet six inches in stature, in the same part of the cellar; they attributed physical paranormal phenomena that took place in the cellar directly to him. This entity was said to be aged in appearance and dressed in rags. The appearance of the so-called "ragged dwarf" has been documented by a number of visitors to Woodchester, and the entity seems to be most active in the cellar.

A Breath in the Dark

It was decided that we would try calling out to Bartholomew or the other entity, the mysterious hooded man. We started with the usual type of questions, completely innocuous and generalized in nature: "Is there anybody here who would like to speak to us?" Linda, Jason, and I all had digital voice recorders running. That's standard practice for us, and with hindsight it would turn out to be a very good thing indeed.

More of us began to ask questions, entreating the spirits to come forward and communicate with us, either by sound or by touch. Another guest felt a hand touching them lightly on the arm.

As we stood there listening to the questions and breathing as quietly as possible, our eyes slowly began to acclimate to the darkness. I could dimly make out the silhouettes of my companions on either side. All of them seemed to be standing as still as possible, keeping the noise down as much as they could.

The breathy sigh took everybody by surprise. None of us were expecting it. It came from just in front of us in the opposite row of investigators. Afterward, we would find out that it came from just behind one of our companions, a harsh guttural noise right in her ear. Quite understandably, she screamed. That, in turn, made the people next to her scream. The panic was contagious, spreading like wildfire among the two ranks, who immediately rushed away from the place where the noise had seemed to come from.

It was sheer pandemonium.

On came the lights. A number of the people from that side of the room were quite shaken up. The three of us were a little irritated at the dramatic outburst but then had to remind ourselves that we weren't dealing with experienced paranormal investigators for the most part; for some of the people with us in the cellar that night, this was their first overnight stay in a haunted location. Small wonder, then, that they had jumped halfway out of their skin when they heard what sounded like a male letting out a prolonged breath directly into the woman's ear.

"Tell me the audio recorders caught that," Jason said, sotto voce.

The three of us formed a huddle, briefly comparing our experiences. Not all of us had heard the exhalation: I certainly hadn't. It was only when we played back the digital recording that it became apparent, a very sinister release of breath. It sounded rather intimidating, as though the intent was to give us all a damned good scare.

Needless to say, it had succeeded.

"Could it have been one of the other investigators playing a prank?" Linda asked, addressing the obvious elephant in the room.

"It's possible," Jason said, but then pointed out that he hadn't seen anybody else moving in the darkness. Everybody had appeared to be standing stock still. He also pointed out that if anybody had broken ranks and moved to growl in the lady's ear, they would most likely have been noticed by the people who were standing next to them. Although the cellar was dark, it wasn't so dark that you could move around in there without being seen. They would also have needed to be extremely quiet, because we hadn't picked up anything in the way of movement on the digital recorders.

Jason floated the idea that maybe somebody had been hiding in one of the empty rooms, somebody who might then have crept forward and been responsible for the growl. My rebuttal was that we had checked the rooms out before the session had begun, and there weren't too many hiding places to be found. Nor could anybody have entered the cellar from the outside, as we were all standing with full line of sight to the staircase that led down from the ground floor. Any intruder would have needed to creep past us, coming within touching distance. It just didn't ring true to me.

We checked the rooms once more, just to be sure. Everything was as it had been before. I resolved immediately that we would come back down to the cellar later that evening and try to get to the bottom of this particular mystery.

"Maybe it's Bartholomew Gilbert," I said slowly, eyeing the old wine cellar. "Sandra did ask him to interact with us. I'd definitely call what just happened an 'interaction.'"

Soldiers

Half an hour before midnight, Jason, Linda, and I made our way up to the third floor of the mansion. We would have it all to

ourselves, and as we crept through the dark and deserted corridors, all three of us were looking forward to working as the
smaller, close-knit group that was our norm.

By the time we'd climbed several sets of stairs and navigated
a maze of empty hallways in the dark, we were out of breath and
excited to get down to work. We picked a spot at random in the
middle of one such passageway, and Jason quickly deployed our
REM Pod at the distant end of the hallway, where it would act
as a sort of sentry, letting us know if any sources of electromagnetic energy were about that we could not see.

We picked out a location to sit, right next to an opening
just off to our right. We were prevented from falling into a big,
empty chamber by a well-placed barrier; this was just one of the
Woodchester Mansion's many sudden drop-offs. Fortunately,
our guide had warned us about the potential safety risk, making
everybody in our group aware of the dangers if we did not take
care when prowling around in the dark.

All three of us recognized the chamber as the place in which
the audience from *Most Haunted Live* had sat. It looked considerably less warm and inviting without the flickering candles and
TV monitors lighting it up.

Once we settled down into comfortable seated positions, the
three of us took turns trying to coax out any entities that might be
present with us, asking them to speak into our voice recorders, approach our K2 EMF meters, or, best of all, touch one of us.

All was silent for the first few minutes of the session. Then
we heard a tapping noise coming from the far end of the corridor, accompanied by what I thought was a shadow moving…yet the REM Pod remained obstinately silent. I wrote it

off as being a simple trick of the light, probably enhanced by my tired and jet-lagged eyes.

The tap came again, above us and off to the right. We all looked up, peering into the darkness overhead but finding nothing. Nor did my infrared camera detect anything unusual up there. Could it perhaps have been one of Woodchester's many bats moving about up in the rafters somewhere?

Tap. This time it was coming from the wide empty room beneath us. Linda and Jason looked down through the gap in the wall, making sure that nobody had entered that chamber. Nothing was moving down there at all.

Thinking of the fact that a number of American and Canadian soldiers had tragically drowned and their bodies brought back to the mansion, I tried to connect with them. "This man was also an American soldier," I said, gesturing toward Jason in the darkness. "If there are any American servicemen with us, would you please come and talk to him?"

"Ooh-rah," Jason whispered.

At first, nothing stirred. Then, *tap.*

The three of us were all looking at one another. We hadn't moved, let alone made that sound. The tap was closer than any of the others had been, yet we still couldn't figure out what it was. Just the natural sounds of an old building settling down for the night... or something else?

We called out again, asking for the answer to one of Woodchester Mansion's most enduring mysteries: Why had the workers all downed their tools and abandoned the place one night? There was no answer, and when we played back the audio recordings later, nothing on there either.

After the initial excitement of the cellar, it now felt as if we were getting nowhere fast.

"I want to get back down to the cellar," Jason said. Linda and I were in complete agreement with him. It had been the most active place so far. This time we wanted to work without a crowd and also try a different technique: the trusty Ouija board.

It was now past midnight, and the three of us sat in the middle of the room from which the disembodied breath had seemed to come. We laid the board out on our laps in front of us and opened it up for use by any spirit who wanted to talk. The stone steps were cool but not uncomfortably so.

The next hour was an exercise in frustration. No matter what we tried—varying our questioning, changing the combination of sitters—we could not get the Ouija board to respond. The planchette barely moved at all. Finally, we had to admit defeat. We resolved to try the board again the following evening at Kielder Castle on the Scottish border. Perhaps the spirits there would be a little more inclined to speak with us.

"Let's switch things up," Jason suggested. "We've tried low-tech. What about high-tech?"

Linda deployed the REM Pod close to the doorway. No sooner had she switched it on and backed away than the device was lighting up, its audible alarm screaming at us. Now that was strange; we had switched off all our electronic devices, so what was causing the sudden flux in electromagnetic energy down there? The basement was deserted apart from the three of us.

The front of the Woodchester Mansion.

We tried to troubleshoot the issue. Low battery? Jason had just inserted factory-fresh batteries. Equipment failure? Linda used the tried-and-tested IT approach of turning it off and turning it on again. The REM Pod continued to alarm, indicating the presence of increased EMF levels, yet there was no apparent source to explain them away. We all stepped away, putting a good twenty feet between ourselves and the device. Still it kept going off.

As quickly as the device had started flashing and wailing, it stopped dead, almost as if a switch had been thrown.

"Do you hear that?" Linda asked, looking all around her in the gloom. "It sounds like breathing."

Jason and I couldn't hear it, but Linda was sure that she had heard the sound of somebody breathing in and out close by. It was coming from a different area than the one in which the two of us were standing, and we couldn't help but wonder whether this was the "phantom breather" that had so spooked the larger group at the beginning of the evening.

Tracking down an explanation turned out to be elusive. The breathing failed to return, and the REM Pod was now on its best behavior. Finally, our guide, Wayne, asked if we'd like to relocate to the ground floor, giving us access to the chapel and the network of rooms and corridors that surrounded it. Up we went, guiding ourselves with flashlight beams, making our way across the building until we reached the area of the chapel, and moving through to the sacristy in the east corridor. Our attempts to generate any activity were fruitless; even the so-called mortuary, which had temporarily held the bodies of the drowned soldiers, was quiet and completely inert at first.

Then the REM Pod came to life again, lighting up and chirping, just as it had done in the basement. We'd already ruled out a possible battery problem. "Could it be one of us?" Jason asked, patting himself down. "I know for sure that my phone is in airplane mode."

Linda and I also had our phones and tablets in airplane mode, but there was only one way to be sure that we weren't the cause of the energy increase. One by one we filed out into the corridor, backing away from the REM Pod. If something about one of our persons was responsible for making it alarm, then putting some distance between us and the device would drastically diminish the effect, as would the thick walls that surrounded it.

The REM Pod continued to alarm.

We stood in the corridor for a few moments, listening to the device screech and watching its lights flash in the empty mortuary. Then, as quickly as if a switch had been flipped, everything stopped once more.

The three of us went back inside the mortuary again, moving up close to the REM Pod. It remained obstinately silent. So much for there being a human cause for the device's strange behavior.

Footsteps

Still discussing possible explanations for the REM Pod alarming, we returned to the break room to enjoy a cup of tea and some snacks. Daybreak was fast approaching, and we had time for just one more session before calling it a night. We all agreed that the cellar seemed to be the most active part of the mansion, and so after finishing our hot drinks, we went back down there in the company of Sandra and several other visitors to try to draw out the disembodied breather that had startled everyone a few hours before.

Forming a loose circle inside one of the larger rooms, we began to call out, inviting any spirit entities present to make contact with us. Shuffling sounds came from out in the corridor. I went out to check, using my thermal camera to see in the pitch blackness. There were no flesh-and-blood visitors whatsoever, whether human or animal (the heat-sensing camera would even pick up something as small as a rat or a mouse), yet when I returned to the circle, the shuffling sounds soon returned, moving just outside the open doorway.

"It feels as though somebody is blowing on my face, right here on my cheek," said one of the visitors suddenly. A number of our colleagues reported feeling extremely cold, a sensation that arose completely out of the blue. There were no drafts, something we had tested for earlier in the evening; were these sudden feelings paranormal in nature, or could they perhaps have been psychogenic, a product of the experiencer's own imagination? It was impossible to tell.

The shuffling returned again. Of course, no perpetrator was found when we went out to check on it. It was hard to shake the feeling that there was an unseen somebody lurking just a few feet outside our circle, watching our every move and listening to every word that was spoken. The skeptical part of my nature wanted to simply attribute that feeling to the fact that we were in a dark basement in a haunted mansion, which was letting my imagination have a field day...but that didn't explain the fact that we all heard the shuffling sounds with our own ears.

Sandra asked whether anybody was willing to go and stand outside in the corridor, or even better to spend some time alone in one of the other rooms. There was a chorus of "No!" and nervous laughter from all around the circle, but one volunteer enthusiastically stepped forward and rose to the challenge: the ever-reliable Jason. I watched his shadowy outline disappear through the doorway, armed only with a digital recorder and a few tools of the trade. He sat down on the cold stone floor outside and invited the spirits to come and interact with him.

"We've all seen horror movies that start like this," I muttered, earning another slightly nervous laugh from the group. It was my hope that the laughter was helping keep up the energy levels in the room, perhaps giving any entities a potential fuel source.

In an attempt to boost the energy levels even further, one of our companions began to play some music, the eerie tinkling sounds of an old-fashioned music box.

"I just heard footsteps out here," called Jason, heading over to investigate. There was supposed to be nobody in the cellar but us, and when he went to investigate, Jason confirmed it. It appeared that our camera-shy spirit visitor was back. At the same time, even more of our companions began to feel cold, yet according to my probe thermometer, the air temperature remained consistent.

Wrapping up at the end of the night, Wayne invited all of us to share our results. We listened with interest as one of the other groups reported having similar results down in the cellar in terms of footsteps and shuffling. One key difference was that this particular group received distinct raps when they asked yes-no questions, including a very definite yes when they asked whether the entity present wanted to be left alone in peace.

It was fast approaching five o'clock in the morning when Jason, Linda, and I stepped outside into the still morning air. I looked up at the glorious night sky, completely free of light pollution, as there were no nearby cities to spoil things, and I took a moment to appreciate the enormous stone edifice of the unfinished mansion that loomed above me. My eyes went from window to window, half-expecting to see a figure looking down at me, one of the many ghosts that are said to haunt this grand old house. They were all dark and empty, however, and as we returned to our car in order to begin the long drive back to London, it was impossible for me to shake the feeling that the Woodchester Mansion hadn't even begun to give up its many secrets.

CHAPTER 7

DROWNING AND BLEEDING

For many people, the phrase *haunted house* will evoke a very specific mental image: an old abandoned castle set high up on a hill, perhaps, or a brooding gothic mansion built on a lonely stretch of moorland.

Brad and I had been friends for over ten years, and in that time we had investigated a number of haunted locations together, thanks to our mutual fascination with all things paranormal. He was a skilled and knowledgeable investigator who was a member of one of our neighboring teams, and I was always happy to see him show up on a case.

For as long as I had known Brad and the rest of his team, stories had circulated regarding a townhome that he owned and rented out to tenants. My longtime friends and colleagues Randy and Robbin swore that the property was paranormally active to an almost unprecedented degree and told countless stories of ghostly activity that had supposedly taken place there over the years.

My reaction to hearing these reports was always the same: "Sounds amazing. Let's go and investigate!" Unfortunately for me, the townhome, located in a quiet suburb on the outskirts of Denver, was usually occupied with tenants, so the opportunity to thoroughly investigate the place never arose. I asked Brad whether the reports of the place being haunted had ever frightened off a renter. He told me that as their landlord, he made it a point never to pry. If the renters were ever to ask him about it (which none of them appear to have done), then Brad would be more than happy to help out; otherwise, he would simply let sleeping dogs lie.

All of that changed in the spring of 2016 when the current tenants moved on to fresh pastures and the property found itself back on the renter's market. I received an exciting phone call one night from Randy and Robbin: Brad's town house was going to be vacant for a week or so before the next set of occupants moved in. Would I be interested in joining them for an investigation there?

Would I ever.

After having spent more than a decade listening to stories about the townhome, I was ecstatic at the prospect of actually spending some nights there. When we arrived for the first night of our investigation, the sun was just going down and the local residents were turning their lights on. The property was located in the middle of a fairly anonymous-looking strip of similar townhomes. From the outside it looked perfectly normal, no different from its neighbors on either side. That, in itself, meant nothing: I had learned through long experience that some of the most haunted residences in the world look just like the house next door.

While I waited for Brad to arrive with the keys, I took a few moments to conduct a walk all the way around the property. This was a technique that I had learned as a firefighter. In the fire service we refer to it as either the "360" or the "scene size-up." No matter how intensely a building might be burning, the wise fire officer will always insist on seeing all four sides of it (or as much as possible) because sometimes the knowledge that is gleaned can be crucial.

With there being other townhomes directly attached to both walls of the property, I really only had the front and rear faces to size up. The front aspect was totally unremarkable, but the rear was a different story. I found a large body of water back there, a little too big to be called a pond. I would learn later that there had been at least one death by drowning there, a fact that would turn out to have surprising implications for the evidence we would gather over the course of our investigation.

Our team for the night consisted of Randy, Robbin, Jason, Linda, and myself. Brad showed up with his adorable pup Raven in tow and unlocked the front door, letting us into the house. Wary of the home's reputation, we stepped inside. It looked ... ordinary. There was little in the way of furniture, but we had anticipated that and brought folding chairs with us. The electricity still worked just fine, but the water supply and air conditioning were switched off, which pleased me greatly; after all, any cold spots or drafts would not be coming from the vents. That was one less thing for us to rule out.

After we had put down our equipment cases in the center of the living room, Brad kindly offered to give us a tour. The home was built on three levels, if you counted the basement. We began upstairs, where we found two bedrooms and a bathroom. For all this time I had been wondering exactly what it was about either the house itself or the ground on which it was built that would explain a possible haunting, and as we were shown around the place, Brad filled us in on what he knew of its history.

Murder—Suicide

The house had been the scene of a particularly tragic murder-suicide, in which a husband had killed both his wife and his young child by drowning them in the bathtub. He had then laid their still soaking-wet dead bodies out on the bed in the master bedroom, before going downstairs to the laundry room in the basement and hanging himself from a pipe.

Brad had corroborated as much of this story as possible from a detective who had been involved with the case. *No wonder this place is said to be haunted*, I thought to myself. The thought of somebody murdering their spouse and child in cold blood was absolutely chilling, and also made me feel very angry at the unknown man for having done such a thing. Yet it was also easy to see how the loss of those three lives in such a violent manner might leave behind a psychic scar of some kind, an imprint on the environment within the house that might be picked up on by those who were sufficiently sensitive.

Broadly speaking, there tend to be three types of haunting: haunted people, haunted objects, and haunted places. We were almost certainly dealing with the third type here. After all, none of the occupants of the house had survived that dark day; the furniture and any other objects that may have been around at that time were also long since gone. That left us with the house itself.

It bears repeating that haunted locations tend to become so for one of two reasons: either somebody loved being there a great deal, feeling a sense of enormous fondness and affection for the place (as is common in many residual hauntings), or more alarmingly, events that caused great pain, anguish, and terror took place there. Either type of event could leave an imprint on a location, and the key seemed to be the depth, intensity, and often the duration of the emotions that were behind it all.

Brad had owned the property for more than ten years, but it wasn't his primary residence; he used it as a rental, leasing it out to various tenants. He rarely broached the subject of ghosts with them (a wise move, in my opinion), but the house had seen a number of occupants disappear before their term was up without offering a word of explanation.

Heading downstairs to the basement level, I noticed a huge gaping hole in the cement floor. Brad explained that he had dug it out himself while working on the sewer line beneath the house.

"I've experienced some crazy activity here myself," he told us as the grand tour reached its conclusion in the basement. I warily eyed the heavy steel pipe from which the former owner was said to have tied his noose. "And it's not just me. People have been touched, shoved, scratched, you name it…We've seen shadow figures, especially on the staircase. Cold spots and drafts even on hot summer days. Voices coming from upstairs and down here when the house is empty."

We all looked at one another, balancing our mounting excitement with a very real sense of trepidation. Many of the cases that I have been called in to investigate over the course of my career have been relatively harmless, with much of the fear factor for the people involved coming from the very natural fear of the unknown that we all have to a greater or lesser extent.

This wasn't going to be one of those cases.

An Angry Spirit

Among members of the paranormal research community, it has become very fashionable to bandy the word *demonic* around these days. The word itself carries some baggage, associated as it is with specific religious belief systems. Although I am not a person of faith in the conventional sense, I do like to think of myself as being spiritual, and I would be a fool indeed to ignore the many accounts on record that speak of contact with inhuman entities—beings that seem never to have walked the earth in human form.

Nevertheless, I do feel that such cases are much rarer than many people like to think. The term has become synonymous with the darker types of haunting, ones in which the entities involved seem to be spiteful and malevolent, wishing the investigators nothing but harm... and sometimes actually inflicting it, causing scratches and other physical wounds to manifest. This happened to one of my novice investigators when we were researching the old Tooele Valley Hospital in Utah, causing a series of angry red scratches to appear on her shoulder blade and upper back.

Needless to say, these types of investigation are rarely pleasant. However, they can also provide some of the most spectacular and fascinating phenomena for those researchers who are willing to stay the course and not allow themselves to be driven away.

I do not believe that all "dark hauntings" are necessarily demonic or inhuman in nature. If we accept the possibility that our spirit may survive bodily death and transition into some form of afterlife—one in which it may still interact with the living in various ways—then it also seems quite logical to me that our personality would remain mostly unchanged too. This tracks with what several psychic mediums have said to me when I have asked them about the nature of the afterlife: we do not instantly become all-knowing, all-seeing, and practically angelic in behavior when we die and leave the body, but rather we retain the same quirks, behavioral characteristics, and essentially the same mental state as we had when our heart was still beating.

Imagine yourself being invisible, intangible, and above all unable to easily interact with your surroundings or communicate with those loved ones that you have lost (or more accurately, have lost you). Imagine the sheer frustration of finding your circumstances so dramatically changed, and not necessarily for the better. Would you be sad?

Bitter?

Angry?

Enraged?

Under those circumstances, I think that a temper tantrum would be entirely understandable. There are a great many angry people walking the earth right now, prone to violence and aggression when they do not get their own way. Why would we expect them to suddenly change their behavior just because they have shed the physical body? I have come to suspect that many of the dark and violent hauntings that are taking place can be attributed to the hostile behavior of dead human beings rather than demonic or inhuman entities. Not all of them, by any means, but a good proportion.

Try putting yourself in the shoes of a man who is so mentally and emotionally unstable that he is capable of not only murdering his own wife and child, but also of then going on to take his own life immediately afterward. Without knowing the details, we can only guess at the troubled state of mind that would be necessary to behave so abhorrently.

What would such a personality do if it felt itself to be threatened or provoked?

We would soon find out that answer for ourselves.

The Ovilus Speaks

Brad elected to stay with us for the first half of the night. Before things got going in earnest, we put our heads together and came up with a plan for the forthcoming investigation. After consulting with Brad, it was agreed that the main hotspots appeared to be the upstairs bedrooms and bathroom. We wanted to monitor those areas in as much depth as possible.

As we were splitting up into smaller groups and gathering up our equipment, Brad told us about the time when a lady claiming to be a psychic medium had visited the house. He had allowed her to wander the premises, following along in her wake. Brad didn't speak, for fear of unduly influencing her, but did carry around a digital voice recorder with which to record every word she said.

Wandering into the master bedroom, the visitor approached the closet and proclaimed that the spirits that haunted the house used it as a portal or a conduit in order to enter our plane of existence.

After she had left, Brad played back the audio file and listened to it carefully for possible EVPs. All was unremarkable until the point on the recording at which the self-professed psychic had made her pronouncement regarding the closet; a female voice, speaking very loudly and clearly, called out, "Faker!"

Brad had invited a total of four mediums to assess the townhome, bringing each one in separately. He made a point of keeping them all in the dark about the history of the house and the findings of the other psychics. When all was said and done, all four told a remarkably similar story: each pinpointed the bathtub as being the scene of a death, and each said that they believed somebody was drowned in there. Another commonality was the sense of there having been a life-or-death struggle upstairs, a floor they all agreed was full of bad feelings and energies.

The first piece of equipment that we fired up was the Ovilus. Among members of the paranormal research community, the Ovilus is a contentious device. Some feel that the device is a useful means of communicating with discarnate entities, whether they be the spirits of the dead or some other type of life, whereas others are convinced that the words spoken by the device are utterly random and completely meaningless.

Speaking personally, for several years I was on the fence where the subject of the Ovilus was concerned... until a number of "direct hits" changed my mind. On one charity investigation at the old governor's mansion in Denver, I walked up to some friends who had been using the device without any success up until that point. Just as I opened my mouth to speak, the Ovilus piped up with the word *paramedic*, which just happens to be my chosen profession. The owner, the same friend and colleague named Randy who was with us in the town house, had made a point of saying that his Ovilus had never spoken that particular word before in its hundreds of hours of operation.

That evening at Brad's townhome, the Ovilus would wow us with a string of spectacular hits that still amaze me to this day. We ran two of the devices at the same time, one owned by Jason and the other by Brad.

Homicide was the first word that came up, followed by *resent* and *them*. Was this just coincidence, we all wondered, or the words of a resentful spirit that was either the victim of homicide ... or had perhaps committed it?

Jason began unpacking his extensive array of recording equipment. Taking a brand-new microSD data storage card out of its packaging, he cursed under his breath when it snapped into two halves. *Geek*, said the Ovilus.

"Did you guys hear that?" Sitting in a chair in the center of the living room, Brad had just heard a woman's voice whisper something indistinct into his left ear. The rest of us shrugged, shaking our heads. We had heard nothing.

From the kitchen came the sounds of slurping as the adorable Raven began lapping at the water bowl that Brad had left out for her. *Dog*, the Ovilus remarked at the same time. This was accompanied by a massive EMF spike on our K2 meter. Considering the fact that we had all set our phones to airplane mode upon arrival and that there was no WiFi network in the building, the source of this sudden energy surge remained a mystery.

In an attempt to make contact with any entities that might be present, Linda began asking questions. She was several months pregnant and had been of two minds about accompanying us on the investigation, but in the end the lure of the location's history had won out. "Who was drowned in the bathtub upstairs?" she asked.

The answer to her question came immediately from the Ovilus: *bath*, it said, followed straight away by *drowned*. We all looked at one another. This was beginning to stretch the boundaries of coincidence a little too far for our liking.

Randy was then next word. Randy raised his eyebrows and leaned forward, interested that his name had come up. *Rob* came right on its heels, possibly short for Robbin. *Bath* was repeated.

"I think that's our cue to go upstairs," Jason said. He, Linda, and I headed on up the staircase while the rest of the team stayed down on the ground floor. We took one of the Oviluses with us, and left the other in the care of Randy, Robbin, and Brad.

Confess! said our Ovilus when we reached the upstairs landing, directly outside the bathroom door. *Bath*.

That was the third time the word *bath* had been mentioned. We were beginning to take the hint. "I'm going to get into the bathtub," I said, switching on the bathroom light and staring down at the tub. It looked . . . well, normal, completely ordinary. Without knowing the history of the location, nobody would ever have guessed that it had been the scene of a double murder.

"Hey guys," Linda's walkie-talkie crackled.

"Go ahead, Robbin," she replied.

"The Ovilus just said, *Hey, upstairs, three*," Robbin told us. Considering that three of us had just come upstairs, it was hard for us to take it as anything other than an acknowledgment of our presence. *Mommy*, the Ovilus said next.

The word was disturbing. Could it have been the spirit of the child, telling us that its mommy had died in the bath? I climbed gingerly into the tub, lowering myself down into a sitting position with my legs stretched out in front of me.

British, was the Ovilus's take on that. Seconds later it was followed up by *British enemy*.

"I'm not an enemy, I'm really quite friendly," I called out to the empty room, trying to keep my tone light and friendly. Knowing what had happened in the very same tub I was now sitting in put a less-than-pleasant slant on things. A few minutes passed in silence. I simply sat there and let the digital voice recorder run.

Drown

From out in the hallway, there came a sudden commotion. I heard Linda and Jason muttering in low voices and hopped out of the bathtub to go and join them.

Linda is an extremely professional investigator, with many years of experience under her belt. I had worked with her on numerous cases and had always been impressed with her grounded approach to fieldwork. All that made what Linda told us next even more remarkable.

She had been standing at the top of the staircase directly outside the bathroom door, which was closed at the time. The hallway was dark, thanks to the lights being switched off, but a little ambient light was coming up from downstairs. Off to the side was the doorway that led to the master bedroom.

Jason had taken up a position in the back bedroom, out of sight but close enough to come running if something strange happened...which it most certainly had. For a moment, Linda had thought that her eyes were playing tricks on her. Something was emerging from the pitch-black interior of the master bedroom. Looking back after the fact, she described it as a dark gray misty form that was perhaps four feet high. Interspersed with the darker background color were a host of lighter patches, which seemed to swirl around and around like wisps of smoke.

The form rushed toward her through the open doorway and then simply disappeared into nothingness, leaving Linda with her jaw hanging open in stunned silence. Jason asked his wife whether she was okay, and Linda replied that she was fine, just a little startled. She was kicking herself for not getting a photograph of the anomaly, but by the time the thought had even crossed her mind the thing had disappeared.

Whatever the misty form had been, it had not triggered any of our sensing equipment. The EMF meters remained stubbornly silent. Only the Ovilus had anything to say about the matter. *Drown*, it added helpfully. It seemed that drowning was starting to become the theme of the night.

The three of us agreed that we had earned ourselves a break. Flipping on the lights, we headed back downstairs. Linda related her experience to Randy, Robbin, and Brad. They had all been to the townhome many times before and had their own strange occurrences to relate, so none of them were particularly taken aback by what had happened to Linda. Robbin, for example, had received a brutal slap across the face from an unseen hand during one of her first visits.

Large British, said the Ovilus, which annoyed me just a little. Yes, I weighed in at a hefty 270 pounds, but was it really necessary to point it out? Assuming that it was an intelligent response rather than a random one, the comment might have been intended in a lighthearted, humorous way. But all of a sudden, the nature of the words coming out of both Ovilus devices took a turn toward the nasty, more violent side of things.

Hit.

Attack.

Blood.

These three words began to repeat themselves. Any idea that we might have had about the communicator being a child (thanks to the *Mommy* message we had gotten earlier) now went out the window. Whoever—or whatever—seemed to be speaking through the Oviluses now was displaying truly vindictive tendencies.

We had best watch our backs. Randy and Brad decided to take a turn standing watch upstairs, leaving the rest of us on the ground floor.

As the night wore on, the messages coming through via the Oviluses became increasingly aggressive and threatening.

Hurt.

Attack.

Beat.

"If you're trying to frighten us, you're doing a lousy job," I said, refusing to be bullied.

Randy, came the response. All eyes turned to look at the man himself. Randy appeared completely unruffled, however. In a weak attempt to lighten the mood, I cracked a joke.

"Randy, huh? I hope that wasn't intended in the British sense of the word." (The word *randy* has sexual connotations to British people that might make others scratch their heads.)

British, the Ovilus shot back. Surely this couldn't be put down to coincidence... could it?

Seeking to stir the pot a little, Linda asked whether the entity had anything else to say to the only Brit in the room.

Exercise.

"Give me a break!" I said, gesturing at my waistline. "That's the second time tonight you've called me fat!" We all laughed. It softened the tension in the room just a little bit.

The K2 meter suddenly shot all the way up to maximum and stayed there for a few seconds before returning to normal once more. I wondered whether our invisible observer was laughing along with us—or at us.

"Do you have anything to say to the redhead?" Linda asked, referring to herself.

Red.

Hurt.

Blood.

Although we tried to laugh it off, most of us found this response pretty disturbing. Red could refer to blood, of course, or the color of Linda's hair. We would not realize until after the investigation was over that the meaning of these three specific words could have been much more sinister and malevolent than they seemed at first.

Feeling less than thrilled at his wife being threatened, Jason made what was possibly an unwise choice: he decided to try and stimulate the entity by calling out that it was weak, pitiful, and not even strong enough to send an EMF meter off the scale, let alone physically injure one of us.

Beware, the Ovilus replied straight away. Thirty seconds passed without anything else happening. Then the K2 meter shot up into the red zone, its maximum sensitivity level, as if taunting Jason in return.

"Do something to one of the guys upstairs," said Linda. A few seconds later, Brad and Randy reappeared on the staircase. From the looks on both of their faces, we could tell that something out of the ordinary had transpired.

When questioned about it, Brad revealed that he had felt an ice-cold hand touch him on the exposed part of his upper left arm, just below the sleeve of his shirt. The fingers had then wrapped around his bicep and slowly begun to squeeze. Seconds later, the same thing happened to his left leg, with the invisible digits taking hold of his calf muscle below the knee. Brad had decided that enough was enough and had come downstairs again.

That wasn't the only unusual activity to take place on the upper floor. Both men were convinced that they had seen twin points of white light in the back bedroom, hovering in one of the corners. The back bedroom was believed to have belonged to the daughter of the house at the time of her tragic death.

After comparing notes, we determined that Brad had gotten touched at almost exactly the same time that Linda had asked the entity to do something to the men upstairs. Getting her dander up, she told the spirit that it really needed to grow a pair.

Big. Ball, was the less than savory response. Under any other circumstances it would have been funny, but we were beginning to get the distinct impression that something in the townhome was playing with us in the same way that a cat plays with a mouse for its own cruel amusement.

Spirit of the Murderer

As we took another quick break and got a little caffeine on board, I began telling my fellow investigators about an interesting experience that I'd recently had at work. I had accepted a job as a tour guide for a very haunted hotel, guiding visitors around some of the historic old building's paranormal hotspots. As a treat for my wife and me, I had booked a room in the hotel for one night after my tours so that we could celebrate my new job in style.

When I woke up the next morning, Laura noticed a large, crescent-shaped scratch mark on my right buttock. It was deep enough to have drawn blood. Considering the fact that neither Laura nor I have sharp nails, I had no idea of just how it could have gotten there. Certainly, it had not been there the night before when we had gone to bed.

I was in the process of showing everybody a photo of the scratch (after all, what's the harm in displaying your naked butt to friends?) when one of the Oviluses called out, *Scratch. Bottom.* Yet again, the boundaries of coincidence had been stretched to the breaking point and beyond.

BOOM! As one, we all looked up at the ceiling. A loud thud had sounded from directly above our heads.

Body. Drop, said one of the Oviluses. Its partner said, *Beware*. At the same time, two of our K2 meters simultaneously flared up into the orange zone, indicating the presence of a strong electromagnetic field.

Body. Drop... None of us particularly liked the sound of that, but we had to check it out. Heading upstairs, we looked around. Nothing had fallen or been disturbed in any way that we could see. We could find no explanation whatsoever for the thud.

"I think we could be dealing with the spirit of the murderer here," Robbin said. "It's hard to believe that either of his victims would act like this."

"You should be sorry for what you did!" Linda said with an edge of anger in her voice. The EMF meters spiked all the way up to red again. *Attack*, said the closest Ovilus.

"What kind of coward would attack an innocent woman and a defenseless child?" I weighed in.

British. Jerk, the Ovilus responded. Guilty as charged!

Next it was Randy's turn. "He's right. You're really pathetic."

Randy. Grab.

It was nothing short of remarkable that the Oviluses had identified each of us specifically—myself by nationality and Randy by name—and targeted a response immediately after we had spoken ill of the entity that we believed was manipulating them. I had never seen anything like it in my entire career.

Things took a turn just a few moments later when I was inspecting one of the devices carefully. *Rest. Mommy.* Those words sent a shiver running down my spine, the sort of thing that a child would say to its mother... or something that was imitating a child might say in an attempt to garner attention.

One thing was for sure: I didn't trust our phantom communicator, not one little bit.

"Where's the little girl?" Linda demanded.

Upstairs.

"What did I see upstairs?"

Tina.

"How old is Tina?"

Four. Upstairs.

This was unbelievable. The answers were coming through the Ovilus thick and fast, almost entirely on demand. It felt almost like a conversation, going back and forth via the medium of an electronic gadget.

"Where am I from?" I asked, changing the subject slightly.

Bath. Jerk.

Yet again I was being called a jerk! Somebody really didn't appear to like me all that much.

Linda asked whether somebody was waiting for us upstairs.

Mommy.

Demon.

And there it was... the *D* word. Was this true, random, or an attempt to incite fear among our ranks? We had no way of knowing for sure. Much would depend on the belief system of the reader, and I leave it up to you to make up your own mind.

Robbin asked whether the entity could make a noise upstairs. As if on cue, the floorboards above our head creaked in the same way that they would if somebody stepped on them—except the upper floor was empty.

Ceiling, the Ovilus added.

Deciding to change tack, Robbin asked whether our invisible communicator could tell us what happens when we die.

Alive!

"Are you reliving the experience of drowning your family over and over again?" Linda asked.

Family.

Things Get Darker

It was getting late, so we decided to take another break. Deciding that he had seen and experienced quite enough for one evening, Brad headed home, taking the adorable Raven with him.

When we resumed our investigation some fifteen minutes later, the Ovilus kicked things off with a blatant threat.

Attack.

Rob.

2. Night.

Even the most skeptical of us raised an eyebrow at this. Attack Robbin tonight—how much clearer could the messages get?

"If you're not careful, we're going to come upstairs and deal with you face to face," Robbin said, completely undaunted by the threatening communication from the Ovilus.

Rob.

Ascend.

Taking this as a direct challenge, our entire group—Randy, Robbin, Linda, Jason, and I—all headed upstairs. As the bathroom was too small for us all to fit inside comfortably, we elected to stake out the child's bedroom at the rear of the house. Once we had all gotten ourselves settled, Linda turned out the lights.

"All right," Jason ordered in his most commanding tone of voice, "Whoever or whatever has been threatening us needs to get its butt up here—right now!"

Order. With. Anger.

The Ovilus had hit the nail on the head yet again; Jason had ordered with anger, which was entirely understandable when one considered that his wife had been threatened. So far tonight, its hit rate was nothing short of incredible.

A loud crash came from downstairs. We had left nobody down there, and Brad had made a point of locking the doors when he left.

"Who is that?" Robbin asked.

Daddy.

Daddy.

"Look at this thing," Linda said, pointing at the Ovilus that now lay on the carpet next to Jason, "It's going berserk."

Cord. Cellar. Choke. Squeeze. Drunk.

Linda asked whether we were talking to the child or her father.

Daddy. Family. Tragic. Hanged.

"This is insane," I whispered, watching in fascination as each new word appeared on the screen of the Ovilus. "Hit after hit after hit. I've never seen anything remotely like this before."

Here. Rest. Pain. Grab.

In what seemed like a reference to the hole that Brad had dug in the cement floor of the basement, the next words were *cement*, *cover*, and *basement*. I had to agree that for reasons of safety, he probably should cover the hole in the basement cement.

Jason asked whether we had heard the true story of the double murder-suicide.

Complete. Error.

Now we were debating just what exactly the truth of the matter was. If we were indeed communicating with the spirit of the father, why would he be motivated to be truthful with us? Particularly as so many of the messages had been full of bile, hatred, and anger, all of it directed toward us.

"I'm beginning to wonder if anybody even died in this house at all," I said, expressing some of the frustration that everybody was beginning to feel.

Mommy. Upstairs. Mommy. Closet. Beware.

The Ovilus continued to spit out an unrelenting stream of woe.

Tragic. Daddy. Very. Horrible. Mommy. Children.

The EMF meter began spiking and dropping at seemingly random intervals. I tried to make sense of the messages. *Mommy* and *Daddy* were both coming up quite often. As for *closet* and *beware*, the implication was obvious: there was something in the small closet that we needed to beware of.

As for the last phrase—*Tragic. Daddy. Very. Horrible. Mommy. Children.*—well, the thought of that was heartbreaking...if it were genuine. I reminded myself that the wise paranormal investigator always took information gleaned from techniques such as this with a massive grain of salt.

Soaked

Things became quiet after that. I wondered whether the paranormal activity was dying down for the night, which is something that we see quite often. It is almost as though a battery had been drained, leaving no energy available for the phenomena to manifest.

"How the heck did that happen? My clothes are soaking wet!" In the darkness, Linda sounded less than happy. Flipping on the lights, we gathered around her to see what she was talking about. A huge oval-shaped damp patch had somehow appeared on her right side, at least one foot in height and perhaps half that in width. It had soaked through the fabric of her t-shirt and jeans but had left her underwear completely dry.

It couldn't possibly have been sweat, otherwise Linda's underwear should have been every bit as damp. Sweat tends to accumulate in the parts of the body that chafe against one another, such as the armpits and inner thighs. In Linda's case, the wet patch was completely lateral, running through the empty hip pocket of her jeans.

Whatever the source of the fluid was, it had to have come from somewhere outside her body. I got down on my hands and knees and began to sweep my palms across the carpet, looking for wet spots in the area where Linda had been sitting. Finding nothing, I broadened my search to cover the entire surface area of the room. Once again, nothing. The carpet was completely dry from wall to wall in every direction.

This made absolutely no sense whatsoever. Dry carpet. Wet clothing. Dry underwear. How does something like that happen?

"Maybe Brad had the carpet steam cleaned recently," Jason said doubtfully. "Some water soaked into the deep fibers?"

I appreciated his willingness to look at it skeptically, but I wasn't buying that as a possible explanation. I'd felt the carpet with my own hands and could confirm that was completely dry. Still, ruling out all possibilities is a large part of our job description.

Fully aware of the indignity of the situation, I lay face down on the carpet in exactly the same spot where Linda had been lying and told Jason to hop up onto my back. He gave me one of the strangest looks I've ever seen and said, "You've asked me to do some strange things over the years..."

"If there really is deep moisture in the carpet, you'll be pushing me down into it with all your body weight," I explained. "Let's see what happens to my clothes."

Which is exactly how I came to have a fully grown male standing on my back at three o'clock in the morning in a haunted bedroom... Let's file that under "reasons I love being a paranormal investigator" and move on, shall we?

After five minutes had passed, Jason hopped back onto the floor and I stood up to allow the others to examine my clothing. It was bone dry. (Brad confirmed the next day that he had not had the carpets steam cleaned.)

Our attempts at coming up with a rational explanation for the wet spot on Linda's clothing all came to naught. We settled for taking photographs of her from all angles, documenting the phenomena as best we could manage.

Things did wind down after that. EMF levels returned to normal and stayed there. The Ovilus devices stopped talking. Finally, a little before five o'clock in the morning, we packed up our gear and went home.

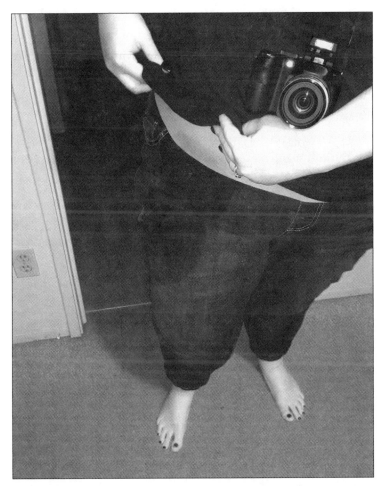

Mysterious patches of water that appeared on Linda during our investigation of a haunted town house in Colorado.

It had been one of the most disturbing cases of my career to date. As I drove home along the interstate, keeping myself awake with a bottle of Mountain Dew and some very loud rock music, my mind kept going back to the damp patches that had appeared on Linda's clothes. No matter what type of case we were investigating, that would have been a fascinating piece of evidence, one that defied easy explanation ... but this wasn't the everyday, average case at all.

This case involved two deaths by drowning, both of them in a bathtub just fifteen feet away from where Linda had had her experience. There was also the reported drowning in the body of water outside the townhomes to take into account. There was a definite aquatic feel to the case, and the fact that water had somehow appeared on the clothing of one of my investigators would have to be quite the coincidence.

But we hadn't heard the last of things. Not by a long shot.

Bleeding

Linda had been investigating haunted locations for many years when she spent the night at Brad's townhome. I had worked on many of those cases with her. She hadn't flinched when we were creeping through the dark corridors of a haunted Southern sanatorium, one in which thousands of tuberculosis patients had died in excruciating pain; she had been equally calm and collected when we had spent the night in a country and western music joint that was claimed by some to be a literal "portal to hell," replete with stories of demonic possession and violent physical attacks (although for us the investigation had been a mostly uneventful one).

My point is that Linda is not remotely easy to spook, and that made what happened to her in the days after the townhome investigation more than a little unusual. Although her personal experiences were not common knowledge among members of the team for quite some time, she has given her blessing for me to share them in this book.

Pregnant with her first daughter, Linda was horrified to discover that she was suddenly suffering the onset of abdominal pain. To make matters worse, it was accompanied by unexpected vaginal bleeding. Fearing the worst, she sought immediate medical attention. Although the doctor was able to reassure her that all seemed well with the child growing inside her womb, the prolonged bleeding was unexplained and a source of genuine concern.

Linda's mind kept going back to that night in the townhome, particularly the cruel and taunting words that kept coming from the Ovilus.

Red.

Hurt.

Blood.

Could this have been coincidence, she wondered, or were her bleeding and pain being caused by a negative attachment from the townhome—one that was messing with the life of her unborn child?

Red.

Hurt.

Blood.

For the very first time in her ghost-hunting career, Linda felt genuinely afraid.

Tell It to the Marines

BCPRS and our friends from the Other Side Investigations went back to the townhome for a second time just a few weeks later. Due to work commitments, I got there in the early hours of the morning, when much of the investigation was already over.

The team included Kira, who had worked with BCPRS for many years and was one of our most experienced, trusted paranormal investigators. Linda had chosen not to accompany the team this time, a decision that I respected 100 percent. If there genuinely was something negative affecting her pregnancy that had followed her home from this location, exposing herself and her unborn daughter to it a second time would be nothing short of reckless.

Some of the investigators had decided to take things to the next level this time, bringing in a Ouija board in an attempt to communicate with whatever it was that haunted the townhome. Such boards can be a double-edged sword, and while many members of the paranormal research community employ them on a regular basis as a means of spirit communication, skeptics like to point out that tiny automatic movements of the muscles can also explain the manner in which the board works.

The team was getting some intriguing results, many of which were less than pleasant in tone. Assuming that they really were communicating with a discarnate entity (rather than their own subconscious thoughts), then we were dealing with a spirit that was extremely hostile, one that meant us nothing but harm.

Upstairs in the master bedroom, Kira and Robbin encountered what they described as a drifting black mass, there one minute and gone the next. It seemed to emanate from the closet that one of Brad's visiting psychics had declared to be a portal of some sort, one that allowed entities to move in and out of this plane of existence. Whether you believed that or not (I personally would require more in the way of evidence, particularly when considering the EVP that immediately declared the medium a *faker!*), there was also the very concerning string of phrases that had come from the Ovilus during our first investigation:

Mommy. Upstairs. Mommy. Closet. Beware.

That sounded one heck of a lot like a warning to me. Had Kira and Robbin just encountered the reason for that warning? When I compared the descriptions afterward, the dark mass that they both reported seeing was strikingly similar to that which Linda had encountered at the top of the staircase, which had come through the master bedroom doorway toward her. Same location, probably the same phenomenon, I reasoned. Was there any part of this house that wasn't paranormally active?

After the second night's investigation, another paranormal investigator experienced something disturbing at home. This time it was Marvin, one of the very dependable researchers that I worked with at many haunted locations in the past. A former United States Marine, Marvin is pretty much unflappable. Having heard about the townhome from Jason and Linda, he had jumped at the chance to investigate it himself. This had also been his first-ever Ouija board session and would definitely be one that he would never forget.

Attachment

Shortly after returning home from the investigation, Marvin realized that something appeared to have followed him back from the townhome. As soon as he walked in the door, Marvin went straight to bed. His wife, Felicia, awoke later that same morning. As she sat at the kitchen table and enjoyed her first coffee of the day, from the corner of her eye, Felicia saw a male figure enter the kitchen.

Naturally assuming that her husband had come back early, Felicia turned around to ask him how the previous evening's investigation had gone—and saw that the figure was nowhere to be seen. Frowning, Felicia got up and went into the bedroom, only to find her husband sleeping peacefully, exactly as she had left him.

When Marvin woke up, Felicia asked whether he had gotten up earlier that morning and come into the kitchen without speaking to her. Marvin shook his head. He had been fast asleep from the moment his head first hit the pillow.

It looked as though Marvin had brought back an unwanted house guest from the townhome.

Things took a turn for the strange around the house after that. Lights all around the home began to flicker, dimming and flaring at seemingly random intervals. They had behaved just fine until the night of the investigation, but now seemed to have taken on a mind of their own. Marvin and Felicia briefly considered the possibility of the wiring having gone bad, but soon dismissed the idea out of hand—what was the likelihood of that happening all at once?

The bedroom door began to open itself when the two were sleeping. Children's toys that were kept for when their family members came to visit began to switch themselves on. One night, while conducting evidence review in his office, Marvin was interrupted by a quick, darting movement from the corner of his eye. Turning to see who it was, he caught sight of a shadowy head darting back around the doorframe, as though its owner had been caught spying on him. Marvin went out into the hallway to investigate and of course found it to be totally deserted.

Finally, Marvin and Felicia decided that enough was enough. They took the rather unusual step of investigating their own home. They broke out a spirit box and began to ask questions, trying to determine who exactly it was that they had seen lurking just out of sight inside their house.

The session wasn't yielding much in the way of results until Marvin asked how the spirit inside their home had gotten there. The answer came immediately through the device's speaker: "Your door."

Marvin initially took this to be a facetious answer. Any human being could flippantly give the same answer and be telling the truth, but when Marvin told me about the response I interpreted it somewhat differently.

"That was your first time ever using a Ouija board, wasn't it, Marvin?" I asked him. He agreed that it was. "What if that's the door that the spirit box was talking about—not literally the door to your house, but the door you opened up during the Ouija session?"

Many regard spirit boards as being doorways into our world from what they think of as the ethereal planes. Had the session that Marvin had conducted at the townhome opened a doorway that allowed someone—or something—to come through and attach itself to him? It could certainly be looked at in that way.

There was no way that the timing of the bizarre activity inside his house was a coincidence.

Marvin had brought something back with him.

The plot thickened even further when he played back the audio recording from the spirit box session. A soft voice could be heard saying the words "Help me." It had not come through the device itself, and had not been heard at the time, but there was no denying that the words had been said.

Marvin and Felicia kicked around the idea of getting the house blessed but ultimately decided to wait things out and see how they developed. Neither particularly liked the idea of sharing their home with a ghost, but they accepted that it was an occupational hazard for those who go in search of the paranormal on a regular basis.

Fortunately, their phantom visitor seemed to lose interest in them after a few weeks, and before long things had gone back to normal in their household. The lights behaved normally once more, and the kids' toys sat silently in their box until it was time for them to be played with.

As for the townhome itself, shortly after the second investigation, it was leased out once again. At the time of writing, it is currently occupied. Brad makes a point of not asking the tenants about any ghostly activity and hasn't received any complaints from them yet. The lease is due to expire in a few weeks' time, and as soon as the townhome is vacant again, BCPRS will be going back to launch another investigation into its haunting.

This chapter does have a very happy ending, however. Linda gave birth to a healthy young baby, who at the time of writing is happily keeping her parents awake at all hours of the day and night. It has not kept Jason and Linda away from investigating haunted houses, I am happy to say, but to this day Linda flatly refuses to set foot in the townhome ever again.

I can't say that I blame her in the slightest.

Would you?

CHAPTER 8

WHOLLY HAUNTED

Over the course of my career in paranormal research, I have spent the night in plenty of locations that were definitely less than comfortable. There was the Hostel, for example, which was ice-cold for the entire five days I spent there and whose roof leaked so badly that rainwater was running down through the light fixtures, threatening to cause an electrical fire. Or what about the so-called Hammer House, scene of the brutal murder of a drug dealer, which was completely open to the elements when my team and I hunkered down there for an overnight vigil?

Yet every so often the pendulum swings in the opposite direction. When reports of a haunted Italian restaurant reached me, images of meatballs, spaghetti, and pasta sprang instantly to mind. Just the mere thought of it made my mouth water.

Add to that the fact that the restaurant was located just a few miles away from home, and the decision to go and investigate was a complete no-brainer. After all, how often did the opportunity arise to eat some world-class Italian food before setting out on one of our ghost hunts?

Wholly Stromboli is situated along the main stretch of Fort Lupton, a small town located just a few miles east of the interstate highway. It wasn't a tough sell to my team ("Hey guys, want to investigate a haunted Italian restaurant?"), so we had a full roster of investigators.

The sun was just beginning to set on a busy Saturday night when the BCPRS team arrived at the restaurant sans equipment, which we were going to leave inside our cars for now. After all, we didn't want to affect business by putting any of the regular customers off.

From the look of things, business was booming. Practically every table in the joint was taken, as were all of the bar stools, where the crowd of early-evening drinkers were laughing and chatting amicably with one another over their beverage of choice.

When I first met with Melissa, the restaurant owner, I was immediately impressed by both her candor and her down-to-earth demeanor. She was friendly and welcoming, ushering our large group to a set of tables that had been pushed together in order to accommodate us. She made sure that a waitress took our order before bustling off to keep an eye on the rest of her clientele, promising to return for an interview once things began to settle down for the night.

We began to relax and settled in for a carbohydrate bonanza that left us stuffed almost to bursting and threatened to send some of our investigators to sleep, victims of the dreaded "carb coma." Thankfully, there was caffeine to counteract that, and as the diners began to drift out table by table, Melissa came over to sit with us. Taking a spare chair, she began to tell us her story.

Realizing a life-long dream to own and operate their very own restaurant, she and her husband had acquired the structure that would become Wholly Stromboli in 2010. The St. John Building, as it was called, was once home to the St. John Mercantile Company. It was so named because it had been owned by a local man named Edgar St. John, someone with whom Melissa believed she had developed an unusual sort of bond.

"We both share the same birthday," she began, searching for the right words to convey her feelings without making herself come across as being a little odd. "I feel drawn to this place somehow and connected to Edgar St. John. It's kind of difficult to explain…"

During their first weeks of ownership, Melissa found herself becoming increasingly preoccupied with the old building. Her interest grew until it began to border on an obsession. Whenever she was out of the house, Melissa would catch herself finding any excuse to drive past Wholly Stromboli, looking in through the windows "just to make sure that everything was all right."

"That brings us to the ghosts," I said, jotting down notes as she talked. "What happened here to make you think that Wholly Stromboli is haunted?"

"I guess it started with little things," Melissa said, casting her mind back. "Employees getting touched when they were all by themselves. Mostly it happens to the women. It certainly happened to me several times; I've been touched on the arm, the leg, and the…" She pointed at her rear end in a slightly embarrassed manner.

That got my attention. No wonder Melissa was less than happy about some of the activity; after all, she couldn't permit the resident entities to goose members of her staff. The fact that all of those affected were female was a little disconcerting. Melissa's own mother felt a sharp tug on the back of her apron one day, which might have been written off as a trick of the mind if it weren't for the fact that an astonished customer also witnessed it taking place.

Things Heat Up

It wasn't long before the paranormal activity became more blatant. Both a staff member and a customer watched a fork flip itself up and off the counter when nobody was within touching distance. In the kitchen, a set of heavy pans that had been stacked on top of the range suddenly crashed to the floor, once again with no living person around to affect them.

Two staff members watched the meat slicer begin to operate itself, its mechanism sliding to life despite the fact that the device wasn't switched on.

At the opposite end of the restaurant from the kitchen was the bar. On one particularly busy night, the bar lights were seen to turn themselves off and on again—although one might be tempted to put this down to faulty wiring, that explanation may not hold water in this case because multiple witnesses saw the switch being physically flipped up and down. (Then again, it must be pointed out that these are patrons drinking at a bar...)

The activity was not confined to the upper floor. Downstairs, the mostly unfinished basement was a place where the staff members didn't like to venture alone if they could possibly help it. An employee was walking through there one evening when she passed through a doorway. Nobody was down there but her. Immediately, the door slammed shut right behind her, giving her the shock of her life; the startled waitress made a beeline for the staircase, wanting nothing more than to leave whatever haunted the basement behind her.

As I scribbled down notes as fast as my hand could write, it occurred to me that we were now entering the realm of poltergeist phenomena. Melissa related the fact that on some mornings, dining tables that had been cleaned thoroughly and set at close of business the night before were found to be dirty and rumpled. Some even had small mounds of salt heaped carefully upon their tablecloths.

One day, as Melissa and one of her employees were cleaning the men's restroom, they watched in utter astonishment as one of the pictures hanging on the wall suddenly hurled itself across the room.

"Are you sure it didn't just fall?" I asked, maintaining a healthy skepticism. Melissa shook her head.

"No way. This didn't fall; it hopped off its nail and flew. We both saw it. And no, before you ask, nobody was pounding on the other side of the wall. The restaurant was empty and quiet."

This made me raise an eyebrow. Flying furniture was something that was difficult, if not impossible, to misconstrue as something else.

Melissa went on to tell me about the time when her set of keys disappeared. She searched high and low for them, enlisting the help of her husband and some of the staff members. They looked through the entire restaurant several times, all to no avail.

At her wits' end, Melissa happened to turn a corner not far from where she thought she had lost the keys, only to find them hanging from the branch of a potted tree. It was as though somebody was either playing with her ... or taunting her.

I was getting ready to suggest the possibility of a prankster among the staff, but the explanation frankly didn't make a lick of sense. No matter how good they may be, unless they happen to be world-class magicians or illusionists, most are incapable of making framed pictures fly across the room or making a light switch flip itself off and on repeatedly.

Perhaps most intriguing of all, an apparition of a young girl—no more than seven or eight years old—was seen hiding beneath one of the tables on several occasions, although when staff went to take a closer look, the apparition was gone.

"I don't want you to stir anything up, make it angry, or intimidate it," Melissa instructed us. "Whatever spirits are here—and I think there are more than one—had to have come with the building. They've been here longer than we have, and I don't want to antagonize them. I just want to find an explanation for all the weird things that have been happening here at Wholly Stromboli."

I for one was glad to hear that. It has been my experience that many people coexist quite peacefully and happily with their residence ghosts, particularly once the fear factor has subsided. I am a big believer in the old saying that knowledge dispels fear, and our overall goal was to help gain that knowledge on Melissa's behalf.

Occam's Razor

On that optimistic note, it was time to kick off our investigation. While Melissa and I had been talking, the team had been busy shuttling in the equipment cases from the parking lot. Now that the last customer had left and the last staff members had gone home for the night, we had Wholly Stromboli all to ourselves.

As two of the most senior investigators, Seth and Kira took on the task of drawing a floor plan and also of getting baseline EMF and temperature readings. Kira is an extremely talented artist, and the act of sketching out a map was far beneath her skill set, but she assumed the responsibility without complaint. Seth walked along behind her, sweeping with a Trifield EMF meter and a thermometer.

One expects to find high EMF levels in certain parts of a building, such as the points at which utility lines come into the structure, and the restaurant was no exception. Seth quickly pinpointed these areas and marked them on Kira's map. EMF can do some strange things to the human brain (at sufficiently high levels it can make one feel deathly afraid, and even induce hallucinations), so identifying these hotspots in advance is crucial to conducting a proper investigation.

Other teammates were busy running cables and setting up remote cameras in the hopes of catching something paranormal in the act of actually happening. They were guided by Melissa, who pointed out some of the more active areas based upon her personal experience. Jeff, Miranda, and Lucilla were baselining the upstairs part of the building and work their way downward. As Seth and Kira worked their way up, the two teams would cross and end up double-checking each other's readings.

Once everything was set up to our collective satisfaction, we all assembled around one of the larger tables, which we were using as a staging point for our equipment cases. A sudden commotion caused us all to look up: one of the paper towel dispensers was whirring, its mechanism unspooling mechanically. Nobody was within fifteen feet of the device, which was triggered by means of a motion sensor under which one was supposed to place their hands.

There was a stir of initial excitement, which Seth quashed by pointing out that a chef friend of his had experienced the very same thing in his own restaurant. I had seen it happen at my firehouse, and it was usually caused by steam from the shower consolidating underneath the sensor and wafting across its sensory field. Falling back on the tried-and-tested principle of Occam's razor (which essentially means when all things are equal, the simpler of two competing explanations tends to be the correct one), we concluded that this was probably a simple case of an overly sensitive sensor, particularly when Melissa told us that it had happened before.

This incident illustrates the importance of maintaining a healthy degree of skepticism when investigating claims of the paranormal. If one is not careful, it is far too easy to set foot on the slippery slope of believing that every creaking floorboard or cold draft is ghostly in nature. Sometimes an odd occurrence is simply that: an odd occurrence, but not necessarily paranormal.

Flashes

A mainstay of our investigative style is the EVP session, and we were all ready to see what Wholly Stromboli had to offer.

While I watched over the team from the central equipment table, Lucilla, her sister Patty (a guest investigator for the evening), Randy, and Brad were accompanied downstairs to the basement by Melissa and Stromboli employee Jen.

Running a digital voice recorder and a combination EMF meter and thermometer side by side, the group kicked off their EVP session. At first, nothing stirred down in the basement except for the occasional cough raised by the ever-present layer of dust that seemed to coat everything down there. Each time this happened, the investigator would mark the tape with a hushed whisper: "That was Brad coughing at 01:56." It made evidence review so much easier afterward, when it was all too easy to mistake a perfectly natural shift in body posture or clearing of the throat for something paranormal.

"Something just tugged at my shirt," Melissa said, reaching back to smooth out her clothing. "I'm not kidding."

Nothing anomalous was registering on any of our instruments. Just in case, however, Lucilla began to take photographs of Melissa and the space around her with a night-vision camera. Uncharacteristically, the camera refused to focus on Melissa no matter how Lucilla adjusted its settings.

Next came the flashes of light. Randy was the first to see one, lighting up the wall in front of him for just a split-second. There was no way that the headlights of passing cars could penetrate the restaurant's basement. Shortly afterward, Jen and Brad reported seeing flashes of light themselves, but this time they were visible against a different wall, one that led into a nearby storage room.

What looked at first to be unexplained light phenomena caught the team's interest, but I'm proud to say that the members of my team are hardwired to always look for a non-paranormal explanation before jumping to a paranormal conclusion. Once the EVP session was over, they set about trying to debunk the flashes of light. They finally worked out that Kira had been taking photographs upstairs and using a flash. She was asked to do so again while the team went back downstairs to watch and wait.

Sure enough, when Kira's camera began to flash, the very same flashes of light appeared on the walls after coming through a small crack in the door at the top of the staircase. The culprit wasn't a ghost at all—it was a Canon.

While Lucilla's team was conducting their EVP session down in the basement, Seth, Kira, Joey, and Robbin had been conducting their own in the room that was used for washing dishes.

After turning out the lights, they set out an EMF meter and several digital voice recorders and began calling out, trying to entice any spirits that might be present to communicate with them. Apart from the occasional low hum of a car passing by outside in the street, all was quiet and still.

"I've just gone cold," Robbin said, wrapping her arms around herself in an attempt to keep herself warm.

"So have I," agreed Joey.

Seth and Kira, on the other hand, felt just fine. A pair of targeted, localized cold spots—or just a cold draft? By the time one of the investigators produced a thermometer in order to check, the sensation had disappeared as quickly as it had arrived.

A few moments passed without incident before three of the investigators—Joey, Robbin, and Seth—suddenly sat bolt upright and swiveled around in their chairs. They all agreed that they had heard what sounded like an exhalation of breath, originating from somewhere in the shadows behind Seth and Joey.

Firing up a flashlight, Joey went to investigate. Of course, nobody was there to find. Any flesh-and-blood person would have needed to creep past me at the equipment table first, and it's highly unlikely that I would have failed to notice them.

It seemed that Wholly Stromboli was waking up.

Seeing Things

Joey would also report hearing a noise that he thought was either a child's cry or the meow of a cat; it was impossible for him to tell which, but he was convinced that he heard it on two separate occasions over the space of just a few minutes.

When the session wrapped up thirty minutes later, it left the investigators with more questions than answers. Was the cold sensation simply down to the airflow in the old building, despite the fact that Melissa had switched off the air conditioning? And had an invisible somebody really let out a breath in the darkness, perhaps in an attempt to induce a little fear among the members of the group?

We discussed these questions over the course of a break, going so far as to use sheets of hanging paper to test the dishwashing room for stray air currents. None were found, and we had made sure that all the doors and windows leading outdoors were closed and sealed as far as possible.

For the second phase of our investigation, Seth and Kira's group elected to head downstairs to what was known as the "coal room." Melissa and Stromboli employee Jen decided to join them, which was fine with the four BCPRS investigators—after all, more people meant that more energy was being added into the mix.

Melissa went first, leading the team down the staircase and through the darkened basement with an unerring sense of direction that came from having made the same journey countless times. The basement was unfinished, the walls completely bare, and the floors stacked with construction materials. Finding themselves chairs, the investigators positioned themselves carefully in a circle, all looking inward at one another.

From a scientific point of view, this session would prove to be relatively unproductive. Although Melissa and Robbin both experienced a feeling of great sadness, we were unable to gather any objective evidence to back up the sensation they were describing. At one point, Joey and Robbin believed that they saw tiny flecks of light in the air above Melissa's head, which can be looked at in either of two ways.

On the one hand, the appearance of dancing lights during low-light conditions is a fairly common occurrence, the result of "floaties" that we have all experienced at one time or another. Floaties are caused by tiny clumps of protein in the back of the eye, which can cast shadows on the retina that tend to be misperceived as being objects located outside the eye itself. It must also be pointed out that the lights didn't turn up on any of the photographs taken by the investigators.

On the other hand, I found it intriguing that the lights were reported by two observers at almost exactly the same time, and we were able to verify that no flash photography was taking place upstairs during this particular session. Could this all be put down to mere coincidence, or was there a less mundane explanation? We hoped that time and further investigation would give us the answer.

A Grieving Woman

While all of this was going on, Lucilla's group had set up shop in the dishwashing room, hoping to replicate some of the prior team's experiences. One of the team members (Brad) would see what he believed were shadows moving in the vicinity of the large steel refrigerator, but none of the other team members were able to see them.

This time Lucilla decided to throw a spirit box into the mix. Interspersed with the background static of the radio frequencies, the box kept repeating the name "Lucy" over and over again— Lucy is the name that Lucilla often goes by, which I found quite interesting. Once again, I had to ask whether this was random chance or something attempting to communicate with us. So far as I was concerned, the jury was still out.

Gathering around the main equipment table, we went over the events of the night so far. I suddenly noticed that Melissa seemed upset—in fact, there were tears rolling down her face. When I asked her what was wrong, she replied that the feeling of sadness that came over her down in the coal room was still affecting her mood.

"I have never liked being in that room," she explained, dabbing at her tears with her sleeve. "I can't shake the feeling that there's a presence in there ... a woman, I think."

"I didn't want to bring this up when we were down there, but I saw a woman standing behind you when we were all sitting in the coal room." Robbin often gets such impressions during her investigations, having developed what may be mediumistic abilities over the years. She tends to keep a low profile where those capabilities are concerned, only referring to them when asked to do so. "And yes, she did look very sad… In fact, I would go so far as to say that she was distraught."

"Do you know why, Robbin?" I asked.

"I get the very strong impression that she lost a child."

Melissa confirmed that there had been a female associated with the building that had indeed lost a child: Edgar St. John's wife, Nellie. Julia, the St. Johns' daughter, had tragically died at the age of seven. No wonder feelings of crippling unhappiness might still be felt years later. It could also provide a very valid reason for a spirit to remain earthbound. The age of the deceased girl matched that of the apparition seen hiding underneath a table in the restaurant upstairs. Was this the apparition of Julia St. John?

This new information dictated my strategy for the remainder of the investigation. The one common denominator in the basement EVP sessions was Melissa herself: she had been down there on both occasions. I wanted to see what happened without her being present. Working on the premise that the female spirit would probably feel more of a connection with other women, I asked Kira and Lucilla to go down to the coal room by themselves and conduct their own session without any male company.

The two female investigators agreed without hesitation. Unfortunately, their session yielded nothing unusual whatsoever at the time—later, we would learn during the evidence-review phase that they had recorded an EVP that seemed to say the words "I would" and another that said, "Give us some time."

When they came back upstairs, everybody was beginning to feel tired. Checking my watch, I saw that it was almost five o'clock in the morning. It was time to call it a day. Yet as I shook hands with Melissa and thanked her for being a gracious hostess, I found myself wondering whether she was the key to the whole thing. Generally speaking, there tend to be three types of haunting: haunted objects, haunted places, and haunted people. Was Melissa the last?

It may have been the case that Wholly Stromboli wasn't haunted at all—perhaps the focus of all this activity was Melissa herself.

If we wanted to figure that out, we would have to come back and dig a little deeper.

Shadow Figure

Two months later, the team went back for a second investigation. I say "the team" because I was unable to attend, due to a work commitment that I couldn't get out of. As it turned out, I should really have tried harder, because things at the restaurant would take a definite turn for the sinister, and I would always regret not having been there.

From the very beginning of the evening, unusual things had happened. Multiple pieces of team equipment (EMF meters, thermometers, and cameras) had experienced unexplained power drains, a relatively common phenomenon at genuinely haunted locations. This has led some to theorize that the energy is being used to somehow assist spirit entities to manifest, acting as a source of readily available fuel. I personally believe that this explanation has a lot of merit.

One of the cameras began to switch itself off, something it had never done before and has not done since leaving Wholly Stromboli. This happened several times, and while it could be put down to mechanical failure, it seems highly coincidental that this would only happen inside the restaurant and nowhere else.

While sitting in the basement in the semidarkness, several bangs sounded from somewhere up above the heads of the investigators. Those who heard them believe that they might have been footsteps. Considering that the upstairs level of the locked restaurant was totally empty, they could not have been caused by a living person.

Joey and Robbin both caught sight of something truly re-remarkable: a tall, adult-sized shadow figure. Joey estimated that it was about twenty-five feet away from them at the far end of the basement.

It would be tempting to dismiss this as a simple trick of the light, but there were two witnesses, each of whom agreed that the figure was crystal clear and fully three-dimensional, as op-posed to the flat appearance of an ordinary shadow. The figure walked from left to right, briefly blocking out the light that was bleeding out from around the edges of a doorframe (the lights in that particular storage room had been left on when the main basement lights were switched off).

Joey is a level-headed investigator and a man who is not given to flights of fancy, yet the email he sent to me the day after the investigation could have been written by an excited child on Christmas morning:

Holy s—! Twenty-five feet away tops! Straight on. I've NEVER seen anything that crisp and clear. It went through the shaft of light from the door, blocking it out. It was 3-f—-D, with D equaling Depth! It wasn't the standard 2D that you see in pictures. It looked just like a team member walking there, but I knew it couldn't have been because it walked through construction equipment on the floor and would have tripped. I wish you had been there to see it. It was f— amazing, I s— you not, sir.

Please forgive the profanity. I include it simply to illustrate just how blown away Joey was by what he saw. Robbin's description of the figure's appearance and behavior matched Joey's down to the very last detail.

Joey also told me that the figure appeared to be a man wearing a suit; it had elongated arms, with hands that stopped at the level of the knees, and no visible feet—the entity's legs tapered off at the ankles.

Robbin had felt on edge from the very moment she first set foot inside the restaurant, which was a very different feeling from the one she had gotten on her first visit just two months prior. "There was definitely something in the air," she would remark later, "and I couldn't shake the notion that we were being watched."

"You're all to blame."

For her part, Melissa also seemed a little tense and nervous. Her mother was present and would accompany the team during their investigation. Along with the BCPRS investigators, Melissa and her mother sat in a circle down in the basement as part of an EVP session...a session that none of those present would ever forget.

Recounting the experience later, Melissa described feeling a steady pressure mounting inside her chest. As the session continued and more questions were asked, the tightness grew increasingly uncomfortable. As a paramedic, the description reminded me of the first symptoms of a heart attack.

Apropos of nothing, she suddenly burst into tears. The feeling of overwhelming sadness was back, Melissa told her companions. "I feel sad—so sad..."

The tears soon became full-blown sobs. Robbin placed a sympathetic hand on her arm in an attempt to comfort and reassure her. "She was one big bundle of nerves," Robbin told me afterward. Yet that sense of deep sadness would soon change, and not for the better.

Melissa's mood went from distress to enraged anger in the space of just a few heartbeats. "F— you!" she growled at Robbin, turning her rage on the woman who was only trying to help her.

"Whoa, woman!" Robbin said, taken aback.

Melissa's mother found it hard to believe the sudden change in her daughter's affect, plaintively asking, "What's wrong with you?"

"I'm mad. So angry!" Melissa growled in a low voice. She felt full of rage, which had come out of nowhere and completely blindsided her. She was breathing heavily, sucking down air in deep breaths in the manner of one who was fighting to keep a handle on their temper. "I'm mad," Melissa said again.

Robbin couldn't help but ask the next logical question. "At...?"

"You. And everybody. You're all to blame."

This wasn't the usual happy-go-lucky Melissa sitting in front of them. She was behaving completely out of character, based on what we knew of her. It was almost as if the BCPRS investigators were now dealing with somebody else entirely.

Robbin maintained a completely calm and professional demeanor, one developed over many years in the nursing profession, but this only seemed to make Melissa angrier.

"I'm trying not to say it," the restauranteur laughed. "F— you!"

Melissa's mother asked her why she was suddenly so mad, but her daughter had no explanation to give. Melissa would explain later that the words were just pouring out of her mouth, in spite of the fact that she didn't consciously want to say any of them.

Things escalated quickly. Melissa's hands clenched into fists. She was zeroing in on Robbin specifically, telling the paranormal investigator in no uncertain terms that she wanted to hurt her, and hurt her bad. No stranger to violent patient encounters, Robbin put a little distance between them in an attempt to de-escalate the situation.

This was the first case that BCPRS had ever worked on in which the investigators had felt physically threatened by a living human being. Safety had to be the first priority. The quick-thinking Brad opened the basement door and switched on the lights, signaling an end to the session, derailing the confrontation before it could deteriorate any further.

With the help of Melissa's mother, the team was able to coax her to accompany them upstairs. Once she was free of the oppressive atmosphere of the basement, it seemed almost as if a spell had been lifted. Melissa slowly returned to her old self.

When all was said and done, she felt terrible about the way she had treated Robbin, apologizing profusely for her bizarre behavior. Her mother emphasized that this wasn't the way her daughter behaved and had been more than a little shocked at some of the bile that Melissa was spewing at a team who had only come in to help.

The team felt that now was an opportune moment to call it a night. They wanted to give Melissa some time to be with her mother and to calm down a little. Although she maintained her poise on the outside, internally Robbin was a little shaken up. She had been directly threatened and needed a little space herself. By mutual agreement, the BCPRS crew packed up their equipment and headed home, much earlier than they had anticipated.

Evidence Review

During the evidence-review phase, a number of potentially anomalous findings turned up on the audio files, including what sounded like a series of extremely deep and sinister breaths recorded down in the basement. All the investigators present maintained that they had not been the source of those breaths. It is possible that one of the team members or their guests were inadvertently responsible, however, so we were forced to discard them as evidence.

Equally ambiguous was what sounded like a child's voice whispering the word *help*. The word unfortunately falls right at the point of the audio track where an investigator happens to be speaking, which makes it difficult to make out whether this is a genuine EVP or a simple case of audio pareidolia—the tendency for us to hear seemingly meaningful patterns in what are really just random noises.

More difficult to write off was a whispered voice that was recorded in the coal room, uttering just two words: *Get out*. A second EVP that completely blew me away when I heard it was recorded when Robbin was attempting to coax whichever entities were present to manifest physically by raising the levels of EMF to the point that her K2 meter would spike. The very definite response, heard by nobody present at the time but as clear as a bell on the audio playback, simply said, "Give us some time ..."

Lucilla discovered an EVP that she believed said "We're scared," once again recorded down in the basement. When I listened to the recording myself, I thought that the anomaly was more of a prolonged exhalation than actual words. This illustrates the highly subjective nature of most EVP recordings, which are open to different interpretations from different listeners.

One thing that we could say for sure: Wholly Stromboli was incredibly active, particularly in the basement. BCPRS and our sister teams weren't done with this particular haunted restaurant. Wholly Stromboli still had more cards left to play.

Aggression

Three years would pass before we returned to Wholly Stromboli. This was partly because of our caseload, but I was also very concerned with the possible risks associated with the case. We had a new roster of investigators, including BCPRS stalwarts

Seth and Kira, the ever-reliable Otis, Jason and Linda, Catlyn, and Charlie. Randy and Robbin accepted my invitation to return, as did Marvin, who would go on to investigate a number of haunted locations with us.

Melissa's behavior during the second investigation had been blatantly threatening toward Robbin; what would happen if the next time there was actual physical violence—could she be pushed toward assaulting one of my investigators? As the director of BCPRS, it was a valid concern, and one that I dared not ignore.

I had overall responsibility for the well-being of my people, and felt more than a little guilty at not having been there on the night when Melissa appeared to be on the brink of harming one of them. Based upon Robbin's description, Melissa had reached a point at which she could very easily have lashed out physically. Any police officer or paramedic will tell you that the point at which a combative person begins to fixate on one single individual (instead of being angry at all of them) usually indicates that the encounter is about to turn violent. We watch for not-so-subtle clues in the aggressor's body posture, such as gritting of the teeth and clenching of the fists—both signs that Melissa had been displaying during her outburst.

Would it be safe for us to be around her again?

Speaking to her about the events of that night, I was fascinated to learn that Melissa had little to no recollection of what she had been saying. She told me that if she hadn't heard her own voice speaking in obscenities on the audio recording, she would never have believed that she was the one who had said those things.

There had been much debate among team members about exactly what had happened in the basement that night. As a group whose philosophy is primarily one of healthy skepticism, we had to consider all angles.

Could Melissa have been acting, we asked ourselves, performing for the crowd in order to make for a good story and generate publicity for Wholly Stromboli? If so, there was nothing in it for her. The subsequent BCPRS case file was never released to the public, and the story itself would not emerge for another four years when the incident was dramatized for the episode of a TV show I appeared in called *Haunted Case Files.* Along with Robbin, Melissa went on the show in person to give her side of the story, which I felt was a brave thing to do.

Contrary to popular belief, not all publicity is good publicity. Having a haunted restaurant is one thing; having a haunted restaurant where one of the proprietors might suddenly fly into a rage is something else entirely.

To her credit, Melissa never attempted to soft-soap her behavior or make excuses. To this day, she seems as genuinely puzzled by the bizarre occurrence as everybody else who witnessed it.

I would also be remiss not to mention the delicate subject of mental illness. Sudden unexplained mood swings can be characteristic of some behavioral disorders; however, Melissa has no such medical history, and had suffered no similar episodes of unexplained rage and memory loss before or since the session in Wholly Stromboli's basement.

According to those who were present at the time (including a highly experienced nurse, who was the primary target of her ire), Melissa displayed no signs of being under the influence of drugs or alcohol that night. If she had been, the chances were high that Robbin would have spotted it from the outset.

All of which brings us to the paranormal explanation. Could Melissa indeed have been influenced by a spirit entity? During the first investigation, Robbin had sighted the mournful woman standing directly behind her down in that very same basement. Melissa had been overwhelmed with sadness then, but the intense anger had not been present. Was it possible that she was empathically picking up on the feelings felt by the spirit of either Edgar St. John or his wife?

This intriguing possibility was foremost in my mind when I arrived at the Italian restaurant for my second overnight investigation.

Footsteps Above

From the outset, we were plagued with the same mysterious electrical battery drains and equipment malfunctions that we had experienced during past investigations. As the basement had seemed to be the hub of paranormal activity in the past, we elected to focus our attention there, paying particular attention to the coal room, which had been EVP Central during our former visits.

When Melissa escorted us downstairs, I was struck by how radically different the basement now looked. The bare concrete floors and exposed Tyvek walls were gone; we found ourselves standing inside a fully furnished function room, with plenty of tables for customers to sit at and an area where bands could perform live music.

Things were relatively peaceful at first. As the night wore on, I began to grow disappointed that Joey and Robbin's shadow figure wasn't putting in an appearance. Nor did the phantom child appear willing to come out and engage with some new playmates. Yet just when it seemed that we were going to leave Wholly Stromboli empty-handed, a coal-room EVP session was interrupted by something totally unexpected.

All talking instantly stopped. We looked at one another, unable to make out each other's features in the darkness. I whispered, "You are all hearing what I'm hearing, right?" Each member of the team acknowledged that they were.

We all heard the unmistakable sound of footsteps walking across the floor above our heads. The sound was faint but clearly audible. This wasn't the heavy tread of a grown adult; it was lighter, more childlike. They crossed back and forth above us.

"Is that Julia playing up there?" Kira asked. I for one suspected that she was right.

Our standard procedure when commencing an investigation is to lock all the doors and windows, ensuring as best we could that nobody would come in from outside to disturb us. This was a genuine concern with a restaurant on a weekend evening, when people walking along the street would often try the door handle in the vain hope of getting some food after hours. That was why we had been scrupulously diligent about securing the building once the last customer had left.

Whoever was walking around up there, there was no way that they were a flesh-and-blood human being.

When we went back upstairs to review the evidence, I wasn't surprised to find that our cameras had failed to capture anybody responsible for those sounds. On the plus side, they had shown up quite clearly on the audio recordings, proof positive that we weren't simply hearing things or letting our imaginations run away with us. Although we didn't capture much in the way of EVPs this time out, the recording of those footsteps made the visit more than worthwhile so far as I was concerned.

As we packed our equipment at sunrise and hauled it out to my parked car, I paused for a moment and turned to look back at the restaurant, halfway expecting to see the face of a playful young girl named Julia peeking out at me from one of the windows. Sadly, that wasn't to be. Wholly Stromboli was still keeping secrets, I knew, not the least of which was the identity of the shadow figure that haunted the basement.

But the story does not end there. When Randy and Robbin arrived home, the sun was already coming up over the horizon. They left their equipment in the car, figuring that they'd unpack it later, and went straight to bed.

No sooner had their heads hit the pillow than a loud crash startled them both. The bedroom doors had been flung open, slamming backward against the walls. They looked at one another, trying to figure out what had just happened. They lived alone, so nobody in the house could have been responsible.

Had they brought back a phantom hitch-hiker from Wholly Stromboli, one who was determined to give them a good, old-fashioned scare? If so, the entity hadn't reckoned on the fact that Randy and Robbin had been investigating for so many years that they had long ago lost their sense of fear.

They simply rolled back over and went to sleep.

At the time of writing, Wholly Stromboli is still very much active. Staff venturing down into the basement have heard the sound of a little girl crying, although she no longer seems to want to put in a direct appearance. At other times she sounds happier, giggling as though playing.

Few employees are brave enough to follow the noises in order to investigate further. Melissa is very much at peace with the spirits that haunt her restaurant. "They were here before I was," she likes to point out, "and it's as much their place as it is ours ... maybe even more so."

So long as the activity is unobtrusive and isn't frightening the staff, a status quo exists between the living and the dead at Wholly Stromboli. The case remains open in my files, and Melissa has my phone number just in case that should ever change.

CHAPTER 9

A LITTLE TOO
CLOSE TO HOME

The Christmas of 2014 was a hectic one, not that that's anything new. Although the paranormal research front was quiet, I had just finished writing my first-ever book, and my work as a paramedic, firefighter, and teacher was keeping me very busy.

As Christmas Eve started to loom closer, things began to wind down on the work front, allowing me to snag some greatly treasured time at home to unwind and prepare for the holidays.

My home is an average one, without much of a history. It was built in 2005, and prior to that the majority of what now constitutes its subdivision was farmland. Nobody had ever died there (I was the first and only tenant) or, to the best of my knowledge, had died on the land. There's no obvious reason for it being haunted... other than my own paranormal pastime, that is.

It was in that final week before Christmas that the weird activity first started. Although I had been investigating claims of the paranormal for almost twenty years, nothing strange had ever happened to me before in any of the places that I had lived. Yes, there were mysterious bumps and thuds in the night, but we quite reasonably put those down to our four mischievous black cats, who liked nothing better than to run around the house chasing one another at two o'clock in the morning.

My wife and I had gone all-out on the outside decorations that year. Being enormous Star Wars fans, our front yard was adorned with inflatable Darth Vaders and other science fiction characters, interspersed with strings of colored lights and illumi-nated blow-up reindeer. It had snowed quite heavily, and the entire garden and front of our house looked truly festive. It be-came my evening ritual before retiring each night to stick my head out of the front door and flip the switch that turned off the yard lights.

Usually on a weeknight, I'm in bed by eleven at the very lat-est. During the holidays, I usually pounce upon the opportunity to stay up a little later and catch up on my reading. A couple of nights before Christmas, I took full advantage of the holiday sit-uation and read until I couldn't keep my eyes open any longer. Putting the book down on my bedside table, I turned off the light and closed my eyes, burrowing under the beautifully warm covers.

After just a couple of minutes, the bedroom was lit up like a ... well, like a Christmas tree. Pinks, purples, blues and whites shone through the closed curtains, dancing along the walls and ceiling. At first I thought that I must be dreaming, but when Laura mumbled about them too, I sat up and blinked.

The lights were still there.

Parting the curtains with a hand, I squinted and looked outside.

The entire front yard, not to mention the fence that ran along the side yard, was ablaze with lights. Running on their electrically powered air fans, Darth Vader and his inflatable minions were waving lightsabers around in the middle of the snow-blanketed garden.

Somebody had flipped the switch on.

It was obvious what had happened: we were the victims of practical jokers. Grumbling, I threw on my dressing gown and clomped my way downstairs. When I opened the front door, a blast of icy-cold air went through me like a knife. Drawing the dressing gown around me more tightly, I stepped out onto the front porch in my slippers, teeth chattering and limbs trembling.

From where I stood, I could see that somebody had flipped the power switch to the on position. All the power cords ran back to one central adapter, which had a rocker on/off switch to control the juice to its many outlets. To turn the power on or off, you had to plug the central adapter into an outside wall outlet and then set the rocket switch to on, which Laura and I did every night when it got late. I took care of turning it off right before going to bed.

I had definitely done so that night. If I had forgotten, I would have noticed straight away when I killed the bedroom light, because the room wouldn't have been remotely dark.

Then I noticed something interesting, something that sent a definite shiver along my spine that didn't have anything to do with the chilly winter night air: there was only one set of footprints leading out through the snow toward the power switch.

Mine.

Snow was still falling, and a pristine white blanket coated the entire garden. There weren't even any animal tracks from the neighborhood cats, dogs, and other critters. Just my own slipper prints heading out to the power switch and back again.

So how had the practical joker flipped on the lights without disturbing the snow? I sighed. Obviously, he or she had to have walked exactly in my footsteps, slowly and with painstaking care to cover their own.

Except … I looked past my truck and toward the end of the driveway. No footsteps could be seen walking up from the street either. My truck had been parked there all day, and its tire tracks had been snowed over.

It was physically impossible for anybody to have reached the power stake without disturbing the freshly fallen snow … not unless they had walked out of my own front door, that is—which was plainly impossible, because it was still bolted and locked when I came downstairs to try and get to the bottom of this mystery.

I flipped off the power switch, went indoors, locked up the house, and went back to bed.

Spiritual Parasites

As I mulled it over the next day, it was obvious to me what must be happening. The power point itself was faulty and must have caused the lights to turn on by themselves when the night air got so cold that it had caused the components inside to contract.

Except … how had the rocker switch gotten flipped?

That night, I turned off the power switch as usual and locked up the house before heading to bed. It had been a long day and I went to sleep fairly early, sometime around ten o'clock.

Just after midnight, I woke up suddenly.

The walls were covered with colored lights again.

These shenanigans continued throughout the course of Christmas week. A pattern began to emerge: the lights would always be turned on just a short time after midnight, by a quarter past at the very latest. I tried replacing the power spike with a different one. It didn't help.

Finally, in sheer exasperation, I put the fact that I am an agnostic to one side. On the 28th of December, I conceded defeat and picked up the phone to call my favorite go-to priest.

Other than being a world-class professional cellist and a Catholic priest, Stephen Weidner is my go-to guy for getting to the bottom of certain ghostly mysteries. He's an experienced paranormal investigator and heads up a small but highly qualified team by the name of AAPI (the American Association of Paranormal Investigators).

Stephen also claims to possess the ability to gain certain spiritual insights into cases by means of meditation. While I can't say for sure whether that is true or not, what I can say is that Stephen's insights have been very close to the mark on more than one occasion, and I have learned to trust his judgment implicitly.

I outlined the events of the past few days to Stephen, who told me that he was about to settle down for his evening meditation. How appropriate that when he got back to me, it was just a few minutes after midnight. The lights had just come on again of their own accord.

"There's good news and there's bad news," Stephen began without preamble. "There are two entities attached to you. The good news is that they aren't malevolent. Think of them as spiritual parasites. The bad news is that they aren't positive either. However, they are easy enough to get rid of, or should be, at least."

"How do I get rid of them?" I was eager to know.

Taking your work home with you was one thing when you worked in an office, but it was something else entirely for a paranormal investigator. To tell you the truth, it was creeping me out more than a little. Although I had spent more than my fair share of nights in some of the most haunted places on earth, well, that was something that I just went out and did. My home, on the other hand, had always been sacrosanct to me.

Stuff like this wasn't supposed to happen to me at home.

"Both of them seem to be mischievous," Stephen explained, "and they're kind of... calling negativity to transform around you both. They also feed off each other. Get rid of one, and the other will follow. Their main source of feeding energy is chaos, anger, and depression."

I took a few moments to process this. I am a clinically diagnosed depressive, and so is my wife. It also has to be said that I can be a fairly angry person at heart. It's a personal failing that I have fought to control all of my life, with varying degrees of success.

If Stephen was right, then these entities wouldn't lack for sustenance.

"Where did they come from?" I asked. "Did they attach to me during an investigation?"

"I get the impression that these two followed you from someone else's home. They've also been around you for a few months now. No, they did not come from an investigation…more likely from a visit to a friend or acquaintance. That's all I was able to pick up on. I don't know if any of that makes sense to you at all. The simple way to get rid of them is the usual." Stephen was putting his foot down now. "Be forceful!" he emphasized. "Go the extra step to banish them from your lives. Do sage, incense, smudging, whatever you believe in. But you'll have to be persistent," he warned me. "These buggers like the energy you guys are feeding them, and they aren't going to go lightly."

Despite the shivers this was giving me, I was nonetheless getting intrigued. "Are we talking human entities here," I asked, "you know, spirits of the dead—or something else?"

"These things have never been human," Stephen corrected me. "They're bottom feeders…chaos makers…emotional stressors. They can be mischievous if given enough energy. The holidays are a perfect time for this. Everyone's emotions are heightened."

I thought about it. What Stephen was saying made a lot of sense to me. Although Christmas was my favorite holiday of the year (mainly because I'm a very nostalgic person), it also brought along with it a great sense of sadness and melancholy. I found myself reflecting on Christmases long gone, lost in the distant past, when I would open presents under the tree as a young boy with my parents and grandparents gathered all around.

All of them were dead now, and it made each Christmas a very bittersweet experience. I knew from heartfelt discussion that Laura felt the same way. Could our painful reminiscences be feeding something paranormal ... and unpleasant?

Suddenly, a new thought occurred to me. I sat bolt upright. "Can they harm my family?" I demanded. "The cats? Greta?" I was referring to our rescue cats (all of them jet black) and my stinky white mutt, who also happened to be the apple of her daddy's eye. I would lose my mind if so much as a hair on one of their heads was harmed.

"No," Stephen denied emphatically. "They're limited in scope and power. Your family and pets are safe. These entities are troublemakers and an annoyance, nothing more."

"So, talk to me about the long-term solution," I pleaded. "What are we supposed to do—fight them off using positive attitudes and the feel-good factor?"

A quote from one of my favorite movie franchises (*Ghostbusters II*), spoken by the mayor of New York City, popped into my brain: "What do you want me to do, go on television and tell three million people they have to be nice to each other? Being miserable and treating other people like dirt is every New Yorker's God-given right!"

To my surprise, that was precisely what Stephen was asking for. "Exactly! If you find yourself overreacting or blowing something out of proportion, think about the emotion and take a deep breath. Think positive. Stop the feeding."

"Will talking to them help?"

"Yes. Loudly, clearly, and above all, repeatedly. Tell them they're not wanted. Tell them to get out."

"Cheers, Stephen."

"You're welcome!"

When we had finished chatting, I was feeling considerably more cheerful…and empowered. Stephen had offered up a very clear (not to mention testable) solution.

"Leave it with me," Laura declared firmly. "I'll have a word with our visitors."

And so she did. What followed was a tongue-lashing of epic proportions, making clear to our uninvited guests in no uncertain terms that they were no longer welcome in our home—or outside it in the yard, for that matter; they had better bugger off sharpish, as we say in Britain, or they really wouldn't like the consequences.

Amazingly, it worked.

That night, the lights remained dark after midnight. And the next. And the next.

They're Back…

Our unwelcome visitors didn't trouble us again after that. Once we had seen the new year in with a house full of friends (ones that we had actually invited), things began to return to some semblance of normality again.

Paranormally speaking, 2015 turned out to be a very productive year. I investigated some of my dream haunted locations, scratching a number of places off my bucket list: Bobby Mackey's Music World, Waverly Hills Sanatorium, the Cripple Creek jail, and Asylum 49 are just some of the ghost hunter's paradises that I was fortunate enough to visit. I also got to appear on my first-ever TV show, flying to Toronto to film season one of *Haunted Case Files*.

When December rolled around again, I had never been readier for a Christmas break. The house had been totally normal all year, despite the best paranormal activity that some of those locations would throw at me and my team.

Christmas was here once more. I had no idea that it would bring the ghosts back with it.

I'm a huge nerd at heart and totally unapologetic about my involvement in science fiction fandom. One of the fringe benefits of attending regular conventions is that I've been fortunate enough to meet more than a few actors and other creative folks from my favorite shows over the years, and I always make a point of getting an autographed photo when circumstances permit.

What I'm not good at, to my shame, is getting those signed photos hung on the wall of my living room. My wife Laura somehow finds the time to get them framed, but hanging them neatly in line with the ones that are already there seems to be one of those jobs that both of us positively hate doing. What tends to happen instead is that the framed photos accumulate in one place waiting to be hung, and that's exactly why a stack of ten were sitting on the ledge directly above the fireplace in December 2015, having been there since the summer.

I was on-duty at the firehouse when I got a text from Laura: *Call me.*

Ducking into a quiet room, I called to find out what was up.

"Those pictures just came crashing down from above the fireplace," she told me anxiously, picking up the phone on the first ring. "They came right down on top of Vlad."

My heart skipped a beat. Now I knew why I could hear a note of genuine fear in Laura's voice. Vlad, one of our several black rescue cats, was at fifteen years the oldest of the bunch. Vlad's cat-chasing days were long behind him; he liked nothing better than to curl up into a little black ball in front of the fireplace and snooze the day away in his own special bed.

As Laura told the story, she had been sitting quietly on the couch, putting together a jigsaw puzzle. Vlad was snoring gently, minding his own business. Suddenly, all ten of the heavy signed photographs that had been stacked on the fireplace above his head fell on him.

Luckily, Vlad didn't have to spend one of his nine lives in order to survive the night. Whether some feline survival instinct warned him I don't know, but Vlad must have heard the photographs begin to slide because the plucky little critter darted out of harm's way just a split-second before the heavy glass frames slammed down onto his bed, shattering in a torrent of broken glass.

Laura let out a cry that was half surprise and half fright, scooping Vlad up into a protective hug. She looked up at the fireplace shelf, now empty, and down to the pile of cracked and shattered glass. Her imagination filled in the rest, horrifying images of what might have been—there was no doubt in her mind that her boy would have been killed, or at the very least seriously injured, if the cascade of wood and glass had landed on top of him.

The frames had sat comfortably in place for months, undisturbed, not slipping or sliding. I wondered if the heat from the fire had perhaps radiated up to heat the bottom of the stack and cause the frames to expand a little, making them unstable. When I came home from the firehouse, I let the fire run for an hour and placed the palm of my hand flat on the spot where the pictures had been stacked.

It was totally cool. *So much for that theory*, I thought, scratching my head. *What caused them to fall?*

"There's no reason for them to have fallen," Laura insisted, as though reading my mind. "It's as though they were pushed..."

The Jawa

Looking back on it with the benefit of hindsight, this was probably the first sign that I may have brought something back home with me.

Still, it was easy to write it off as being "just one of those things," and Laura and I soon pushed it to the back of our minds and got on with the business of planning Christmas.

The next incident would prove to be impossible to ignore.

One night a week or so later Laura and I were both fast asleep at around one o'clock in the morning. Laura's eyes suddenly flew open as she awoke with a start.

"Tell that damned monk to get the hell away from me!" she growled, waking me up too.

"Monk?" I mumbled, bleary-eyed.

Laura sat up and turned on the light. The bedroom was empty apart from the pair of us and our still-snoring pooch, Greta.

Laura told me that something had awakened her just a moment ago, some sense that there was somebody else in the room along with us. On opening her eyes, she saw a dark, hooded figure standing over her at the side of the bed.

"It looked just like a Jawa," she said, describing the robed desert scavengers from the Star Wars movies. "And it was short, like they are. If this thing was standing, it was only three or four feet tall, max."

"Did it have a face?" I asked, fascinated. "Eyes, at least?"

She shook her head. "Not even eyes. Just a black space under the hood where the face should have been ... It was featureless ... totally empty."

I looked around the room again, half fascinated and half anxious. My heart was pounding hard and fast in my chest. It was one thing to go out and look for phantom figures in supposedly haunted houses—but it was something else entirely for them to come and find me in my own bedroom! That wasn't how this was supposed to work ...

Calling for Backup

The following morning, I found myself considering the events surrounding the hooded figure from every possible angle.

In the cold light of day, the most obvious explanation was that Laura had experienced a hypnopompic hallucination. This is a condition in which somebody is asleep but is starting to transition toward wakefulness—they are basically partly asleep and partly awake, in other words, and undergo some sort of sensory experience that feels paranormal in nature. This can include hearing voices or footsteps, feeling a sensation of pressure on the body, a sense of paralysis ... or seeing apparitions.

These episodes, along with their cousin the hypnagogic hallucination (which takes place when you are falling asleep rather than waking up), occur more commonly than many people realize. Have you ever mistaken that dressing gown or bundle of clothes tossed casually over the back of a chair for a ghostly figure in the night? Welcome to the realm of hypnagogia and hypnopompia, when your own senses like to tell you ghost stories.

Yes, I decided, that was probably it. Laura had experienced nothing more than a hypnopompic hallucination of a short, hooded figure when she just happened to be waking up in the middle of the night. That had to be it ... right?

Fast-forward two more days. Laura had a job interview coming up, and her focus was on doing her very best to nail it. The afternoon interview was to be conducted by phone rather than in person, and so Laura spent the morning before it wandering around the house with her phone in her hand, trying to find the room in which the acoustics would be the very best possible.

She was in the upstairs guest bathroom.

"Hello," she said. "Hello. Hello."

"Hello."

The reply hit Laura like a slap in the face, stopping her dead in her tracks—mainly because she hadn't been expecting any response at all. The house was completely empty (except for the critters), yet Laura had heard the clear and distinct voice of a woman talking back to her, coming out of thin air.

Greta, our ten-year-old mutt, had been lying in her customary spot on the upstairs guest bed, watching the world go by outside. As soon as the mystery voice spoke, Greta went berserk, leaping down from the bed and tearing downstairs as though all the hounds of hell were on her heels. She skidded to a halt on the wooden hallway floor, where she went totally rigid and began growling and barking at the empty air right in front of her.

"What did the voice sound like?" I asked Laura when I arrived home from work later that day.

It sounded like an older woman, she told me; the voice seemed to originate from somewhere outside the bathroom, with her best guess being the downstairs hallway that led to the front door of the house.

"The voice wasn't angry, or scary, or even remotely creepy," Laura said. "In fact, it was very matter of fact. It wasn't quite polite either; more like the basic courtesy you'd get if you nodded at a stranger and said hello to them."

Christmas was only a week away. As I mulled over the current set of strange happenings that were taking place in my own home, a quote from Ian Fleming's *Goldfinger* came to mind: "Once is happenstance. Twice is coincidence. The third time it's enemy action." In other words, the three unusual events—picture frames, hooded figure, and now the disembodied voice—strongly suggested that there was more going on in our home than mere coincidence.

I picked up the phone and called my friendly neighborhood priest.

"What's up?" Stephen sounded jolly, as befitted the season. "Long time, no talk!" We hadn't seen each other since we both worked together on a charity investigation of a haunted old opera house in Longmont at the end of October.

"Stephen, I think there's something going on in my house," I said without preamble. I recounted the three instances of what I was growing increasingly convinced were paranormal activity. He listened without interruption, and I could easily imagine him nodding gravely at the other end of the line.

"It does sound like it. Have you tried smudging? Telling whatever it is to leave?"

"Not yet. Laura tried that last Christmas, and it worked like a charm. This feels…different, though. I'd like to try some heavier spiritual artillery, if you know what I mean."

He laughed, recognizing the irony of an agnostic asking for the priestly equivalent of an air strike.

"We can manage that. My schedule's pretty hectic, especially around the holidays." Stephen had a number of musical commitments. "The soonest I could make it is Sunday the 27th."

"The 27th would be perfect." I made a note in my day planner. We agreed on a time of two o'clock in the afternoon. The plan was for Stephen to come in and conduct a blessing to begin with. He could always upgrade to a higher level of expulsion later, if the situation warranted it.

Laura and I were both reassured, knowing that there was now a plan on the table.

"Now listen up," I said, calling out to thin air the next day. "If you're here, you have to realize that you're in our house, and that means that you have to abide by our rules." It felt faintly ridiculous to be talking to nothing, but I'd done it many times over the years, with varying degrees of success. "That means no messing with us or, more importantly, messing with our pets. If that was you with the picture frames a while back, you could have hurt Vlad very badly. Not cool. If there are any further attempts to harm, or even just to frighten, anybody in this house, we're going to throw your ass out of here so hard that you're not even gonna bounce. Are we clear on that?"

I waited in silence for a few minutes, half-expecting the disembodied female voice to answer.

There was nothing.

One afternoon five days before Christmas I was sitting quietly on a chair in my hallway, talking to my boss on the phone. Suddenly, as I was chatting away and looking at Greta snoozing on cushions beneath the window of my office, I saw a human-shaped shadow flit across the front hallway from left to right.

It stood out in stark contrast to the white paneling of the front door. I practically dropped the phone in shock, blinking my eyes repeatedly (as if that would help them see more clearly!) and staring at the door in sheer amazement.

The shadow figure had only been there for an instant, but I had seen it as clear as day. There was nobody else in the house to have cast a shadow ... at least, nobody physical.

I sighed. It wasn't necessarily a sinister thing. Perhaps it was simply the entity's way of acknowledging that yes, it was still here. On the other hand, perhaps it was just going about its business and wasn't even aware of my presence, in the same way that I'm generally not aware of the hundreds of people that I pass by on the street every day because I'm too wrapped up in my own thoughts.

Then Laura saw a shadow figure herself, just five feet away in my office. It passed fleetingly through the room as she was working on the computer.

"Oh, wow!" was her startled reaction. "It's you again!"

That was an assumption, of course—one shadow figure looks very much like another—but a reasonable one. It appeared that despite our stern warning, whatever had attached itself to us or our home wanted to keep making its presence felt.

Christmas came and went in the usual way, full of festive good cheer, fine company, and way too much food that was bad for us. No further ghostly activity took place, but it still seemed wise to continue on with the blessing. Stephen arrived at three o'clock on Sunday the 27th, carrying in an old-fashioned leather case that looked rather heavy.

"What's in there?" I asked, intrigued. Stephen plunked the case down on top of the dining room table and flipped the catches.

"Cleaning supplies," he answered with a smile. It turned out that he was only half-kidding. Sitting next to his Bible and prayer book inside the case was a spray bottle of holy water, along with several holy oils and religious accoutrements. Gathering the tools of his trade, Stephen said, "We'll start on the top floor and work our way down. Do you have a basement?"

I nodded. It was full of books, junk, and stored Christmas decorations.

We traipsed upstairs and started in the master bedroom. Dispensing holy water, Stephen talked under his breath, moving from room to room and marking the sign of the cross above each doorway and window frame. When I asked, he told me that he wasn't sensing anything out of the ordinary anywhere in the house.

Stephen repeated the process downstairs, moving from the living room fireplace where the pictures had fallen back toward the hallway area and office where Laura and I had seen the shadow figure.

"Really?" he asked at one point, gesturing up at a framed photo hanging on the wall. I grinned sheepishly.

"Is this the first time you've blessed a house that had a picture of the Antichrist in it?" I asked. As a collector of film and TV memorabilia, I had bought the autographed photo of Harvey Stephens, the child actor who had played Damien in the original movie version of *The Omen*, at a charity auction. In the picture, Damien is standing in the middle of a graveyard and smirking at the camera in a really sinister way.

"Surprisingly, yes," Stephen replied drily, rolling his eyes. The son of Satan got no extra attention during the blessing, though, and before long we were finishing up the ceremony down in the basement. Every room, doorway, and window in my house had been blessed. Even for an agnostic such as myself, it felt like I had called in a spiritual artillery strike.

"What now?" I asked, once everything was complete.

"Now you go back to your lives," Stephen answered, snapping the case firmly shut. "If this entity isn't gone, or if things go from bad to worse . . . call me."

In my experience, reports of paranormal activity tend to die down after Halloween and then spike again over Christmas. Part of that may be due to the fact that fictional ghost stories and the holiday season go hand in hand—*A Christmas Carol* by Charles Dickens springs to mind—but I also like to think that there is a more heartwarming explanation.

Christmas is a time for family and kinship; for gathering together during the long, dark nights and celebrating. Ever since I relocated to the United States in 1999, I have missed those gatherings a great deal. Now that my parents and grandparents have passed on, their absence leaves a big hole in my life that can never be filled. I feel it most acutely during the holidays, especially in

December, when memories of happy Christmases long gone tend to come flooding back.

I have heard several psychic mediums say that our loved ones are never closer to us than they are during the holidays, particularly Christmas. While I'm not qualified to say whether this is true or not, I definitely find myself talking out loud to my lost loved ones during the holidays, letting them know that they are missed and that I wished they were here to share seasonal joy with me, Laura, and our family of critters. It never fails to bring a bittersweet tear to my eye.

The shadowy little figure that Laura had seen seemed highly unlikely to be one of my family members, however, something that Stephen had confirmed during his visit. After calling in the heavy artillery by bringing in my favorite priest to bless the house, I was hopeful that the activity would cease and that peace would return to my home.

I had no idea when the new year came around that life was about to deal me a very cruel blow indeed, but one that would be softened ever so slightly by one last sign from the other side ...

A Last Goodbye

For the Estep household, 2016 started very badly. The apple of my eye had always been my dog, that white-haired mutt named Greta. Everybody who met Greta simply adored her—they just couldn't help it; born with a deformed airway that left her big, floppy pink tongue hanging from the left side of her mouth, she also had soulful brown eyes that radiated love and happiness with every glance, not to mention being wickedly effective tools when she was begging for treats.

Twelve years is a relatively long lifetime for a dog, but as anybody who has ever been honored with the privilege of being a "dog's human" knows, their lives are always so terribly short when measured against our own. Throughout the final months of 2015, Greta became sick with what the vet finally determined was long-term kidney failure.

Laura and I nursed her throughout her decline, but we had to face the dreadful truth that some of the infirmities which accompany old age simply cannot be reversed. At the end of January I was scheduled to fly to England in order to spend a week investigating an old witches' prison in Essex. The vet's opinion was that Greta might be here when I got back, but it was most likely that she wouldn't live that long, as she had declined significantly in the early new year.

With my heart in my mouth and tears streaming down my face, I kissed Greta on the head, hugged her, told her that I loved her more than life itself, and headed to the airport, leaving her in Laura's loving and capable hands. My plans simply couldn't be canceled, and I have never wanted to fly home to England less in my entire life.

A few days later, a tearful Laura called to let me know that Greta had passed in her favorite place, lying comfortably on her pillows in front of the low window in my office. The office is at the front of our house, close to where I had seen the shadow figure flit across the hallway a few weeks earlier, and she had liked nothing more than to perch there for hours, barking at any neighborhood doggies who had the temerity to pass within fifty feet of her turf. Laura and I had fought a losing battle against cleaning off her snoot-marks from the window pane, because usually within moments of wiping the glass down, Greta would have her nose pressed firmly to it again, howling indignantly at yet another encroachment upon her territory.

As one might expect, I fell apart emotionally when I heard that she had passed. Oh, I was able to remain professional during the hours of my investigation, but coming back to my hotel room that first night after hearing the news, I broke down and wept for what must have been hours. I was far from home and hadn't been there at Greta's side when she went to sleep for the last time, although Laura had made sure that the last words she heard were "your daddy loves you more than life itself" and then gave her a kiss on the nose as I had always done.

Squinting to see through eyes that simply refused to stop crying, I said my own farewell to Greta there in the hotel room and then made a plea to any family or friends that had passed over into spirit to go and meet her at the Rainbow Bridge, to look out for her, and give her lots of love until the day that we would finally be reunited. Both of my parents and all my grandparents had passed on, so I knew that my entreaty would not fall on deaf ears.

Unbeknownst to me, Laura was employing that proven age-old strategy of coping with a bereavement: staying relentlessly busy. She embarked upon a house-cleaning of epic proportions, which happened to include cleaning Greta's nose marks from the office window one final time, and then before going to bed she pulled the blinds all the way down to the window-sill. Heartbroken, she realized that there was now no four-legged neighborhood watch scheme operating out of our home office.

Which only made what happened the next morning all the stranger. Laura awoke early and wandered downstairs to make coffee. Carrying the hot, steaming cup into the office with the intent of checking her email, she suddenly stopped dead in her tracks and came perilously close to spilling it everywhere in shock.

The office blinds had been opened and now sat neatly some two feet above the window-sill, at just the perfect height for an inquisitive dog to keep an eye on the world outside.

It seemed that my plea had been answered: somebody was looking out for my Greta after all, and the world suddenly seemed a little less dark.

AFTERWORD

I've learned a great deal following the trail of terror across America and the United Kingdom, and despite undergoing many hours of tiredness, boredom, and disappointment, those times when we seem to be in contact with energies that conventional science doesn't yet understand make it all worthwhile.

It is the curse of the paranormal investigator that for every answer dug up, three more questions rear their heads, often clouding the waters and providing more uncertainty rather than clarity. It is rather like wrestling with a monster—much like the mythical Hydra of Greek mythology, lopping off one head simply causes the beast to grow two more.

Yet if I'm making my passion for all things paranormal sound unfulfilling, I'm doing it a major disservice. After all, why would a relatively sane grown man spend countless hours staking out allegedly haunted locations if the experience wasn't rewarding in some way?

There are few professional paranormal investigators working in the field any longer. I use the term *professional* in the sense of "people who do this for a living," as I have encountered many researchers who apply very professional standards of behavior to their investigations. This is one of the few areas of scientific endeavor where the man and woman in the street are doing all of the heavy lifting, rather than some (but by no means all) of the PhDs who rarely descend from their ivory towers and dirty their hands with field work.

When the big breakthroughs in the field of paranormal research finally do come (and take my word for it, they will come one day), the majority of the work will have been done by those people who give up their free time in order to do it, conducting investigations at night and on weekends, sharing their results freely with their fellow enthusiasts.

One of the locations that I have written about in this book—30 East Drive, the Black Monk House—is basically an ongoing experiment, with hundreds of people rotating through there each year, all of them drawn by the allure of making contact with something not of this world. Some of the evidence being gathered is truly extraordinary ...

And it is growing.

I would like to thank you, the reader, for accompanying me on this journey through some of my favorite cases. Many of the EVPs that you have read about in these pages are posted over at my blog, which can be found at www.richardestep.net. Whether you are an active paranormal investigator, an armchair enthusiast, or even a hard-core skeptic, I would very much like to hear your

thoughts on this book. Please feel free to email me at richard@
richardestep.net.

Now if you will excuse me, I have to go and figure out
what's going on with the blinds in my office...

ACKNOWLEDGMENTS

My heartfelt thanks go out to the following people, without whose kind assistance these adventures would never have happened and this book would never have been written:

Aiden Sinclair, illusionist extraordinaire and conjuror of (usually) false ghosts, for writing the foreword. Don't tell the guests I'm really from Detroit...

My wife, Laura, and her grandmother, Doris M. Smith, for loaning me a well-protected Ouija board.

My fellow Cripple Creek prisoners, Colton Tapia, Matt Laughlin, Shaun Crusha, Aurthur McClelland, Debbie McClelland, Catlyn Keenan, Kindra Stewart, and LaDawn Colescott Stuart.

Michelle Rozell, the nicest prison warden I've ever met.

Andy Yates, and his lovely girls Imogen and Grace, who baked us the nicest cakes we've ever had when we were investigating the Hostel.

Lesley Bridge, paranormal investigator and tea wallah, and her other half, Dave, for opening the doors at London Underground.

Gaynor Clarke, whose pothole avoidance skills left something to be desired.

Hazel Ford and her team from Haunted Happenings, a first-rate group of paranormal tour guides if ever there was one.

Nat Wilson of Haunted Evenings, who froze her arse off with us inside the Hostel and stayed not only professional but also cheerful throughout.

My friends at East Drive Paranormal: Carol Fieldhouse and her daughter Kayla, Claire Cowell, Eileen Hill, Angie Cowlishaw, Scott Hill, Phil Bates, and Jason Lindsay, for generously sharing their time and personal experience.

My brother Matt Estep, who set foot inside not one but two haunted houses to spend time with me—love you, bruv.

Stephen Weidner, a superb paranormal investigator and one heck of a cellist.

Historian Mike Covell, who was kind and gracious enough to share the fruits of his research concerning 39 De Grey Street.

Jason and Linda Fellon, a pair of the truest friends, for countless hours spent together at haunted locations.

Barry Oakley, whose encyclopedic knowledge of the London Underground's ghost stories was both fascinating and invaluable.

Bil Bungay, who trusted a virtual stranger with the keys to his haunted house and told me to have at it.

Charlie Stiffler, whose fault it was that our five nights in Pontefract were rechristened the Search for Stiffler's Monk.

Andrew Cooper, who stopped watching *Star Trek* just long enough to join us at 30 East Drive.

Andy Evans, paranormal investigator and author, whose book *Don't Look Back in Anger* should be required reading for anybody contemplating a visit to the Black Monk House.

Steve Hemingway, paranormal investigator, who dropped by to lend his expertise.

Ray Canham and the Woodchester Mansion Trust, for allowing me to tell the story of their beautiful historic building.

Wayne Spurrier, Michele Hayward, and Carolyn Lee, for handling a gaggle of ghost hunters like a pro and making it all look so easy in the middle of the night.

Brad, Randy "Grampire" Schneider, and Robbin Daidone, for many years of friendship and comradeship.

Kira and Seth Woodmansee, who have helped shape BCPRS since its earliest days.

Melissa Rickman, for letting us tell her story and that of her restaurant.

Joey Stanford and Lucilla Giron, who did sterling work at Wholly Stromboli and on plenty of other cases too.

Mark Maxwell, a great guy to spend time with, whether it's in a haunted firehouse or inside a burning building.

Win Ferrill at the Denver Firefighter's Museum; Ann Leggett, for letting the firefighters of today interact with the firemen of the past; and Shane Rogers, for strong work on his very first case.

My Asylum 49 family in Tooele, Utah, especially Kimm and Cami Andersen and Dusty Kingston. Love you guys and can't wait for Halloween!

The tour department at the historic Stanley Hotel, my fellow ghost nerds and Estes Park family, not to mention friends of the spirits of the Stanley.

And last but by no means least, a big thank you to all of those who have shared my haunted journey over the course of the past twenty-two years. I could never have done it without you!

To Write the Author

If you wish to contact the author or would like more information about this book, please write to the author in care of Llewellyn Worldwide, and we will forward your request. Both the author and publisher appreciate hearing from you and learning of your enjoyment of this book and how it has helped you. Llewellyn Worldwide cannot guarantee that every letter written to the author can be answered, but all will be forwarded. Please write to:

Richard Estep
⁄ Llewellyn Worldwide
2143 Wooddale Drive
Woodbury, MN 55125-2989

Please enclose a self-addressed stamped envelope for reply,
or $1.00 to cover costs. If outside the U.S.A., enclose
an international postal reply coupon.

Many of Llewellyn's authors have websites with
additional information and resources.
For more information, please visit our website at
http://www.llewellyn.com.

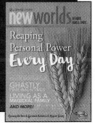

SPIRITS
OF THE CAGE

TRUE ACCOUNTS
OF LIVING IN A
HAUNTED
MEDIEVAL
PRISON

RICHARD ESTEP &
VANESSA MITCHELL

Spirits of the Cage
True Accounts of Living in a Haunted Medieval Prison
RICHARD ESTEP AND VANESSA MITCHELL

The jailer's evil spirit torments residents. The demonic black entity appears in broad daylight. The ghost of a trapped child still searches for her mother.

These examples are just a taste of the terrifying phantoms and tortured souls that dwell in the Cage, a cottage in Essex, England, that was used to imprison those accused of witchcraft in the sixteenth century. When Vanessa Mitchell moved into the Cage, she had no idea that a paranormal nightmare was waiting for her.

From her first day living there, Vanessa saw apparitions walk through her room, heard ghostly growls, and was even slapped and pushed by invisible hands. After three years of hostile paranormal activity, Vanessa moved out, fearing for her young son's safety. Then paranormal researcher Richard Estep went in to investigate. *Spirits of the Cage* chronicles the time that Vanessa and Richard spent in the Cage, uncovering the frightening and fascinating mysteries of the spirits who lurk within it.

978-0-7387-5193-1, 312 pp., 5¼ x 8   **$15.99**

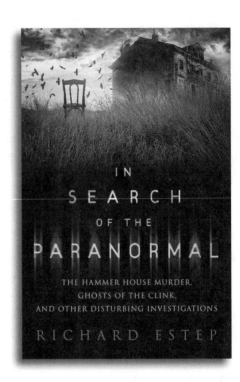

IN
SEARCH
OF THE
PARANORMAL

THE HAMMER HOUSE MURDER,
GHOSTS OF THE CLINK,
AND OTHER DISTURBING INVESTIGATIONS

RICHARD ESTEP

In Search of the Paranormal
The Hammer House Murder, Ghosts of the Clink, and Other Disturbing Investigations
RICHARD ESTEP

From exploring the Tower of London to investigating a haunted Colorado firehouse, paranormal researcher Richard Estep takes you behind the scenes for an up-close-and-personal encounter with a fascinating legion of hauntings. This collection reveals some of the most chilling, captivating, and weird cases that Richard has investigated over the past twenty years, in England and in the United States.

In Search of the Paranormal is filled with rich historical detail, present-day research, and compelling eyewitness accounts. You are there with the team at each haunted location: walking through a desecrated graveyard, shivering in a dark basement, getting thrown into The Clink, watching a "ghost-lit" stage in an old theater. Employing a variety of investigative methods—from high-tech gadgets to old-fashioned practices such as dowsing, table tipping, and Ouija boards—Richard Estep and his team uncover the dark mysteries of the paranormal realm.

978-0-7387-4488-9, 264 pp., 5¼ x 8   **$15.99**

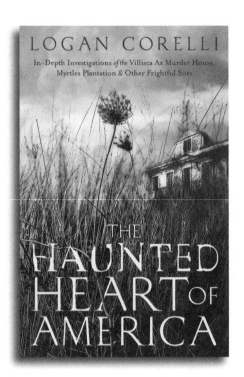

LOGAN CORELLI

In-Depth Investigations *of the* Villisca Ax Murder House,
Myrtles Plantation & Other Frightful Sites

THE HAUNTED HEART OF AMERICA

The Haunted Heart of America

*In-Depth Investigations of the Villisca Ax Murder House,
Myrtles Plantation & Other Frightful Sites*

LOGAN CORELLI

In the heartland, tales of grisly deaths and unsolved murders abound—and the spirits of the dead are often left behind. Join Logan Corelli and his teams as they explore some of the creepiest haunted locations in America, where spirits and entities terrify even the most experienced investigators.

The Haunted Heart of America provides tantalizing evidence of realms of existence beyond our own. Featuring firsthand investigations of famous paranormal hotspots like Waverly Hills, Myrtles Plantation, and the St. James Hotel—as well as many lesser-known though equally fascinating locations—this riveting book shares spine-chilling stories, hair-raising experiences, and amazing physical evidence.

978-0-7387-5591-5, 240 pp., 5¼ x 8   **$16.99**

Stalking Shadows
The Most Chilling Experiences
of a Paranormal Investigator
DEBI CHESTNUT

If the world of the paranormal were a house, *Stalking Shadows* would be its wicked basement. And like a basement full of sinister energy, this collection of true stories is powerful enough to snuff out your flashlight, leaving you trembling in the darkness.

Join psychic medium and paranormal investigator Debi Chestnut as she explores twelve terrifying true encounters with ghosts, dark beings, and negative entities. Discover an abandoned house of horrors that becomes more evil with every victim it claims. Follow a tortured spirit trapped in a forsaken mirror. Feel the savage pain of a distraught ghost that screams out in agony. Once you descend into the paranormal basement, you'll uncover the true lives of the dead—in thrilling ways you never expected.

978-0-7387-3943-4, 216 pp., 5³⁄₁₆ x 8   **$15.99**

Exploring the Paranormal History
of America's Deadliest War

GHOSTS
— *of the* —
CIVIL
WAR

"Rich Newman's compelling new book . . . is the best way to visit over
160 spine-tingling haunts of this most tragic of American conflicts."
—JIM HAROLD, HOST OF *THE PARANORMAL PODCAST*
AND AUTHOR OF *TRUE GHOST STORIES*

RICH NEWMAN

Ghosts of the Civil War

Exploring the Paranormal History of America's Deadliest War

Rich Newman

The Civil War left behind unforgettable stories of brave soldiers, heartbroken families, violent battles … and a paranormal legacy that continues to fascinate and scare us more than 150 years after the war ended.

Paranormal investigator Rich Newman presents over 160 different locations with reported supernatural activity related to the Civil War. Explore major battlefields, smaller skirmishs, forts, cemeteries, homes, and historic buildings teeming with ghosts. Discover the rich history of these Civil War locations and why so many souls linger long after death. Featuring terrifying, heartbreaking, and captivating ghost stories, this book helps you uncover the supernatural secrets of America's deadliest war.

978-0-7387-5336-2, 336 pp., 5¼ x 8   **$15.99**

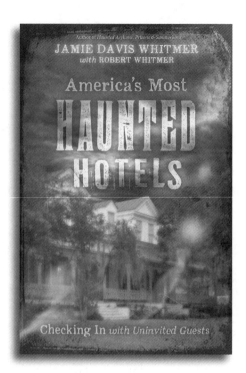

Author of *Haunted Asylums, Prisons & Sanitariums*

JAMIE DAVIS WHITMER
with ROBERT WHITMER

America's Most
HAUNTED
HOTELS

Checking In *with Uninvited Guests*

America's Most Haunted Hotels
Checking In with Uninvited Guests
JAMIE DAVIS WHITMER WITH ROBERT WITMER

Journey into the mysterious world of haunted hotels, where uninvited guests roam the lavish halls, phantom sounds ring throughout the rooms, and chills run along the spine of anyone who dares to check in for a night.

Join Jamie Davis Whitmer, author of *Haunted Asylums, Prisons, and Sanatoriums*, as she explores nine of the most haunted hotels across America. From the Myrtles Plantation in Louisana to the Palmer House in Minnesota, these hotels are discussed in stunning detail, covering everything from the building's history and legends to firsthand accounts of paranormal activity that happened there. You'll also find photos, travel information, and everything else you need to plan your own visit to these haunted locations.

978-0-7387-4800-9, 264 pp., 6 x 9   **$16.99**
